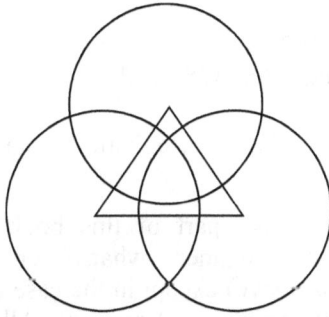

# MATRIX OF AFRICAN PROVERBS

## The Ethical and Spiritual Blueprint for True Civilization based on African Proverbial Wisdom Teachings

By Sebai Dr. Muata Ashby
Edited by
Dr. Karen Dja Ashby

Sema Institute/Cruzian Mystic Books
P.O. Box 570459
Miami, Florida, 33257
(305) 378-6253 Fax: (305) 378-6253

First U.S. edition © 2009 By Reginald Muata Ashby

The author is available for group lectures and individual counseling. For further information contact the publisher.

Ashby, Muata
MATRIX OF AFRICAN PROVERBS: The Ethical and Spiritual Blueprint for True Civilization
ISBN: 1-884564-77-1

Library of Congress Cataloging in Publication Data

## Other books by Muata Ashby

*See catalog in the back section for more listings*

# TABLE OF CONTENTS

# TABLE OF FIGURES

## TABLE OF TABLES

# About the Author

Biography of Dr. Muata Ashby

Mr. Ashby began studies in the area of religion and philosophy and achieved a doctorate degree in these areas while at the same time he began to collect his research into what would later become several books on the subject of the African History, religion and ethics, world mythology, origins of Yoga Philosophy and practice in ancient Africa (Ancient Egypt/Nubia) and also the origins of Christianity in Ancient Egypt. This was the catalyst for a successful book series on the subject called "Egyptian Yoga" begun in 1994. He has extensively studied mystical religious traditions from around the world and is an accomplished lecturer, musician, artist, poet, painter, screenwriter, playwright and author of over 50 books on yoga philosophy, religious philosophy and social philosophy based on ancient African principles. A leading advocate of the concept of the existence of advanced social and religious philosophy in ancient Africa comparable to the Eastern traditions such as Vedanta, Buddhism, Confucianism and Taoism, he has lectured and written extensively on the correlations of these with ancient African religion and philosophy.

Muata Ashby holds a Doctor of Divinity Degree from the American Institute of Holistic Theology and a Masters degree in Liberal Arts and Religious Studies from Thomas Edison State College. He has performed extensive researched Ancient Egyptian philosophy and social order as well as Maat philosophy, the ethical foundation of Ancient Egyptian society. In recent years he has researched the world economy in the last 300 years, focusing on the United States of America and western culture in general. He is also a Teacher of Yoga Philosophy and Discipline. Dr. Ashby is an adjunct professor at the American Institute of Holistic Theology and worked as an adjunct professor at the Florida International University.

Dr. Ashby has been an independent researcher and practitioner of Egyptian Yoga, Indian Yoga, Chinese Yoga, Buddhism and mystical psychology as well as Christian Mysticism. Dr. Ashby has engaged in Post Graduate research in advanced Jnana, Bhakti and Kundalini Yogas at the Yoga Research Foundation.

Since 1999 he has researched Ancient Egyptian musical theory and created a series of musical compositions which explore this unique area of music from ancient Africa and its connection to world music. Dr. Ashby has lectured around the United States of America, Europe and Africa.

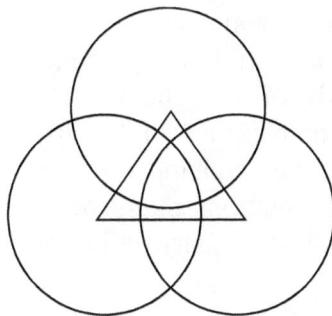

# PREFACE

## What is a *matrix*?

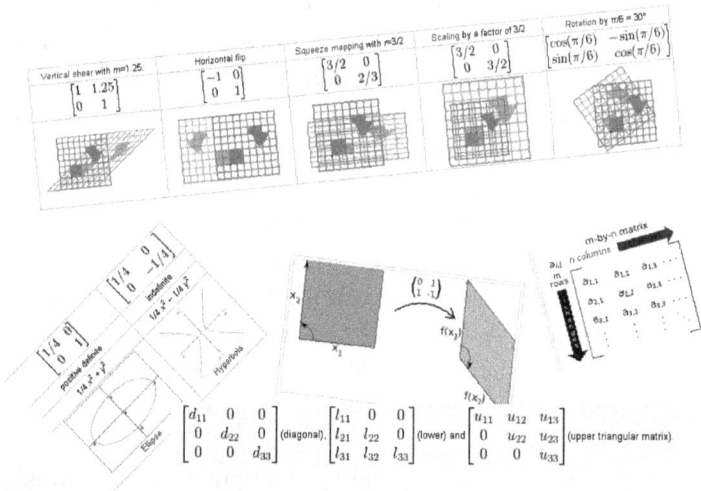

**Figure 1: Mathematical ideas about a matrix.**

cientists have tried to conceptualize, in mathematical terms, what a matrix is, and how to define it. This may be a valid pursuit for scientific inquiry, and may lead to some discoveries. From a cultural studies, philosophical perspective, the study of a matrix is more practical and simple. However, in some ways, it is more intellectually, experientially and emotionally demanding. When we consider the study of what human existence, life, nature and all of the complexities of the world along with the complexities of the human mind and heart are, the mathematical computations might be easy by comparison. Let's begin with the dictionary definition of the term.

**ma·trix[1]**

> something that constitutes the place or point from which something else originates, takes form, or develops: The Greco-Roman world was the matrix for Western civilization.

**ground substance**
n.
1. The intercellular material in which the cells and fibers of connective tissue are embedded. Also called *matrix*.

**ma·trix** (mā'trĭks)
n. *pl.* **ma·tri·ces** (mā'trĭ-sēz', māt'rĭ-) or **ma·trix·es**

1. A situation or surrounding substance within which something else originates, develops, or is contained: *"Freedom of expression is the matrix, the indispensable condition, of nearly every form of freedom"* (Benjamin N. Cardozo).
2. The womb.

In several cultural traditions, there are mythic stories about divinities who weave a matrix of Creation, and as they do so, they spin out and control the complexities of Creation and human life. For example, the Moirae (the "Fates") of Greece control destiny. In Ancient Egypt the goddess Net {Neith} was known as the weaver who weaved the matrix of Creation in which all life exists, and through which the drama of human existence is played out. If this were true, it would mean that the ordinary way that most human beings live their lives is in ignorance of the grander reality of life. That would mean that the true nature, purpose and goal of life is hidden from most people. That ignorance of an underlying matrix (subtle reality of life) causes disorder, conflict and suffering in life. Many who discovered this higher reality found it useful to record their wisdom in the form of proverbs that would promote conditions for that higher reality to be discovered, and also their insights that promote the understanding of it.

Before getting to the proverbial wisdom, let us explore this idea of a matrix and allow that to be a foundation to lead us into the *African Proverbial Wisdom Teachings* that will expound and instruct us about it. A matrix is a foundation upon which something is created. It is also a framework or structure upon which a construction can be based. The

11

matrix is a guide. The question of this study is what are the ideas and principles that African culture and society has been based on from time immemorial? In terms of African society and civilization, the matrix is *proverbial wisdom teachings*. *African Proverbial Wisdom Teachings* are aphorisms and or didactic literature containing instruction in wisdom about worldly and spiritual life that may be found in African cultures from ancient to modern times. These *African Proverbial Wisdom Teachings* embody a uniquely African perspective of life, social organization and spiritual existence, which has been refined and encapsulated over generations. *African Proverbial Wisdom Teachings* contain the guiding principles that were used by ancient African societies, and which can still be found in use throughout Africa. They allow for the transference of wisdom containing a code for the architecture of a well ordered society, and also wisdom for personal, material, and spiritual fulfillment for society as well as the individual. This volume is dedicated to outlining those principles embedded in *African Proverbial Wisdom Teachings* for those who want to recapture the innate African acumen for creating political and economic well-being and spiritual connection to the universe.

At the heart of the African proverbial wisdom is the ideal of relationships of the individual with the spiritual world and the physical world, which if carried on properly, lead to the maintenance of the integrity and balance of society, which in turn facilitates the fulfillment of an individual's purpose in life and death as well. *African Proverbial Wisdom Teachings* are a matrix or framework upon which a society can create laws and regulations to govern everything from family interactions, community relations, including local and national government, as well as economic systems. That original matrix of African Proverbial Wisdom has experienced much change and distortion throughout the last 1,500 years due to social, political and economic changes throughout Africa. However, this volume is dedicated to rediscovering and outlining the ideals and fundamental elements of the social, political and spiritual matrix contained in the *African Proverbial Wisdom Teachings* a as means to clarify the principles for anyone wishing to pursue social, political and spiritual order based on original African principles of good village organization, social responsibility, and personal connection to other human beings, the universe and Spirit.

We may think of the elements of culture that are presented in *African Proverbial Wisdom* as a blueprint for the architecture of a well ordered society that can qualify as a true "civilization," such as was evidenced in Pre-Dynastic Ancient Egypt, which endured high civilization for over 5,000 years. Consider that Western culture is only just over ?? years old and the current state of world affairs threatens the survival of humans and earth itself. If we think of a blueprint as a detailed outline or plan of action, a blueprint for success, the wisdom in African Proverbs shows the elements or components that comprise a blueprint for successful human life and human social interaction. If we think of architecture as the art and science of designing and erecting, we can see *African Proverbial Wisdom Teachings* as a blueprint for how these components of life [varied relationships, interactions between a human being and the world, and the responsibilities of a human life] can work in harmony for the betterment of the society and the individual. This blueprint will allow the construction of a successful individual existence and collective architecture of human civilization.

This volume will look at these architectural components [varied relationships, interactions between a human being and the world, and the responsibilities of a human life] and see how they fit together for the construction of a true civilization that functions in a coherent and lucid, as well as sustainable, fashion. So, taken as a whole, *African Proverbial Wisdom Teachings* may be considered as a blueprint for the architecture of real civilization. The consideration here is not only in terms of technological

13

advancement, but perhaps more importantly, in human development as well, because if the human being is developed properly, then that human being will develop and use technology in a way that would be constructive, rather than destructive. Thus, if applied correctly, it can serve as a manual containing step-by-step instructions for creating a foundation for positive human existence and the social institutions for elevating culture and human professional and spiritual development. This means that instead of being forever caught up in the vagaries of life, the whims of egoistic personal desires, the tyranny of the powerful or the ignorance of self-serving religious leaders and politicians, there is an alternative. The alternative is following the path laid out by sages who traveled the road already and left their insights for posterity, knowing that societies go through cycles of ethical and spiritual heights and lows. In the low times, the teachings serve as a guide, a roadmap, to find the way back to the heights of civilization in yester times.

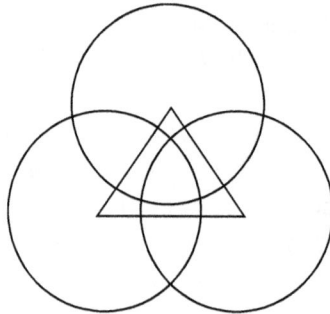

# INTRODUCTION: PROVERBIAL FOUNDATIONS OF AFRICAN ETHICS

*The wise one is a [teacher] to the nobles.*
*Those who know that he knows will not attack him,*
*No [crime or injustice] occurs when a wise one is near;*
*justice comes to them distilled,*
*In the form of the sayings of the ancestors.*
*Copy your fathers, your ancestors,*
*See that their wise words endure in books,*
*Open them and read them, copy their knowledge,*
*they who are taught become skilled.*
-Ancient Egyptian Proverb

Her-Heru, regarded as the first Priest King, and Queen Netchemet reciting a hymn to the Rising Sun (c. 1050 B.C.)

**T**his volume sets forth the fundamental principles of African ethics and their practical applications for use by individuals and organizations seeking to model their ethical policies using the Traditional African values and concepts of ethical human behavior for the proper sustenance and management of society. Furthermore, this book will provide guidance as to how the Traditional African Ethics may be viewed and applied, taking into consideration the technological and social advancements in the present. This volume also presents the principles of ethical culture, and references for each to specific injunctions from Traditional *African Proverbial Wisdom Teachings*. These teachings are compiled from varied Pre-colonial African societies including Yoruba, Ashanti, Kemet, Malawi, Nigeria, Ethiopia, Galla, Ghana and many more.

African Ethics is an important part of African Philosophy. It includes a tradition comprised of *African Proverbial Wisdom Teachings,* a set of written and oral traditions that impart traditional values that were shared by most indigenous peoples throughout the African continent. These teachings formed the backbone of the civilized cultures of African societies prior to the advent of colonialism and the breakdown of civilized cultures throughout Africa. African Philosophy was developed by the peoples who lived and created civilizations in the continent of Africa before Europeans, Arabs and others brought colonialism and other conquering forces, including missionaries, or divergent cultural values, into Africa.

In earlier times, indigenous Africans populated the entire African continent, including North Africa, the Sinai Peninsula and parts of Asia Minor. Today, North Africa is almost completely populated by people of Arab descent. Presently, the vast majority of those on the continent of Africa who still speak indigenous African languages, follow indigenous customs, observe African myths and legends, and practice indigenous African religion and philosophy, are located in the region south of the Sahara desert.

## Figure 2: Religions of Present Day Africa

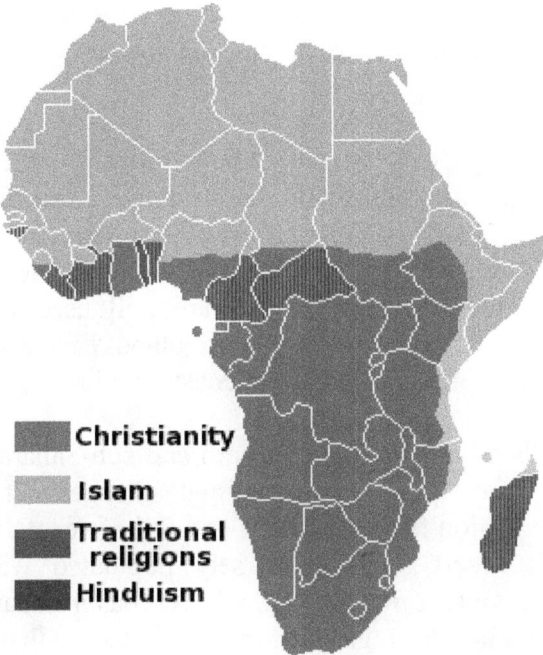

Christianity
Islam
Traditional religions
Hinduism

A map of the Africa, showing the major religions distributed as of today. Map shows only the religion as a whole excluding denominations or sects of the religions, and is colored by how the religions are distributed not by main religion of country. Where overlap, majority is displayed *except* for traditional religions practiced in a syncretic fashion.

The term **"Sub-Saharan Africa"** relates to the geographic area south of the Sahara desert [see green area in the front cover picture of Africa of this book]. This term denotes the countries of Africa that generally are not considered as part of North Africa. The term "North Africa" may now (late 20th and early 21st Centuries) also be expanded to include some areas, such as northern Nigeria and Ghana and other areas in West and Central Africa, due to a predominant change from indigenous African culture to Islamic culture in those areas. In the 19th Century, many Europeans referred to sub-Saharan Africa as "Black Africa" and "Dark Africa," or to Africa as the "Dark Continent." The assignment of the terms was partly due to the dark skin of the indigenous inhabitants, and also because much of Sub-Saharan Africa had not been explored and fully mapped by Europeans.

Those terms ["Black Africa" "Dark Africa" or the "Dark Continent"], are presently considered as obsolete, derogatory, and offensive. Another term, "African Uplands," has been devised to substitute for the derogatory terms, but the derogatory terms are still used in some quarters. Yet, the phrase "African Uplands" mostly refers to the African interior, and not to coastal regions.

After the last Ice Age, the Northern and sub-Saharan parts of Africa were separated by the climate changes that altered the Sahara region from populated and full of vegetation to a dry harsh desert climate, sparsely populated with low vegetation. Over time, the Nile River basin became the only place in the region (northeast Africa) that could support life. The inhabitants of the ancient region that was then forested, but is now called the Sahara desert, migrated north, east, west and south. It has been determined by climatologists that it was no later than 10,000 B.C.E. to 7,000 B.C.E. that there were any substantial rains in that area of the world.

Most of Africa, including *sub-Saharan Africa,* is within the tropics. The term "Tropical Africa" is an ecological term relating to the location of the land territory on earth which lies in the tropical region of the planet. This would exclude South Africa if strictly applied, because South Africa lies outside the Tropical zone.

The reference to Sub-Saharan Africa in one way relates to the ecological situation because the Sahara desert separates North Africa and Sub-Saharan Africa. However, the term also has ethnically and culturally applications, because North Africa is now populated predominantly by people of mostly Arab descent whose ancestors came to that region from Asia Minor [Arabia], and who speak the Arabic language and practice Arabic culture. The Arabs who conquered North Africa [including Kemet (now called Egypt)] moved there after the early conquest period of Islam [rise of the caliphate (632–750 A.C.E.)] following the inception of Islam by the Prophet Muhammad. Previous to that period, most of the inhabitants of North Africa were native Africans who resembled the population of the south. They were culturally and ethnically related to other native Africans and not to Arab or European ethnic groups or cultures. Some scholars and politicians classify the present day North Africans as "Caucasoid." However, the "Caucasoid" and or "Arab" populations that currently reside in North Africa often possess swarthy and other "Africoid" type physical characteristics due to "miscegenation"[2] with the indigenous "black"[3] Africans that originally resided in the region. Nevertheless, while there may be some differences in appearance between the peoples of Arab descent in North Africa from those in Asia Minor, the North African Arabs follow the predominant culture, language and religion of Asia Minor [Arab-Islamic] more closely than any other.

> "Our people originated
> at the base of the mountain of the Moon,[4]
> at the origin of the Nile river
> where the god Hapi dwells."
> -The Ancient Egyptian tradition

The Nile valley was the only region of North Africa where life could flourish because the Nile provided regular floods that facilitated farming. In ancient times the peoples of that region, sometimes referred to as Nilotic (encompassing an area along the Nile river from Uganda at the source of the Nile, to the outlet of the Nile River into the Mediterranean), migrated north and created civilizations that were later referred to as Kush (Ancient Ethiopia) and Kamit (Ancient Egypt, also Kemet, KMT)

> *"They also say that the Egyptians are colonists sent out by the Ethiopians, Asar having been the leader of the colony. For, speaking generally, what is now Egypt, they maintain, was not land, but sea, when in the beginning the universe was being formed; afterwards, however, as the Nile during the times of its inundation carried down the mud from Ethiopia, land was gradually built up from the deposit...And the larger parts of the customs of the Egyptians are, they hold, Ethiopian, the colonists still preserving their ancient manners.*
>
> -Recorded by Diodorus
> (Greek historian 100 B.C.)

It has been adequately demonstrated by many scholars that the Ancient Egyptians were indigenous African peoples, in other words, dark-skinned, "black" Africans.[5] The importance of this finding will become clear as we proceed with our studies of African Proverbial Wisdom. The following accounts from ancient Greek writers describe the physical characteristics of the Ancient Egyptians of their time.

> *"The **Egyptians and Nubians (Ethiopians) have thick lips, broad noses, wooly hair and burnt skin...**
> ...And the Indian tribes I have mentioned, their skins are all of the same color, much like the Ethiopians... their country is a long way from Persia towards the south..."*
>
> -Herodotus

**Figure 3: Herodotus, the "father of history", wrote that Egyptians had black skin and woolly hair.**

*"the flooding of the Nile could not be caused by snow, because the natives*

20

*of the country (Egypt) are black from the heat".*

-Herodotus

*"And upon his return to Greece, they gathered around and asked, "tell us about this great **land of the Blacks called Ethiopia.**" And Herodotus said, **"There are two great Ethiopian nations, one in Sind (India) and the other in Egypt."***

-Recorded by Diodorus
(Greek historian 100 B.C.)

Dialogue:

*Lycinus (describing an Egyptian):* **'this boy is not merely black; he has thick lips** *and his legs are too thin...his hair worn in a plait shows that he is not a freeman.'*
*Timolaus:* **'but that is a sign of really distinguished birth in Egypt,** *Lycinus. All freeborn children plait their hair until they reach manhood...'* *(Lucian, _Navigations_, paras 2-3)*

Dialogue:

*Danaos (describing the Aegyptians (Egyptians)):* *'I can see the crew with their **black limbs** and white tunics.' (Aeschylus, _The Suppliants_, vv. 719-20, 745)*

*The Egyptians were **"very black"** and the Ethiopians **'wooly haired."***

(See Aristotle, Physiognomy, Chap. VI).

*As for the people of India, those in the south are like the Aethiopians in colour, although they are like the rest in respect to countenance and hair (for on account of the humidity of the air their hair does not curl), whereas those in the north are like the Aegyptians.*

- Strabo, Greek historian, geographer and philosopher

21

"the northern Indians are most like the Egyptians physically".
-Arrian, Greek historian

**Figure 4: Strabo wrote that the Egyptians resembled the people of northern India.**

Given the ethnicity of the Ancient Egyptians and the evidences about their origins from continuous contacts with Africans of the interior of Africa, the Ancient Egyptian culture, religion and philosophy should be considered as a part of the family of African cultures, religions and philosophies.

## African Wisdom for All Humanity

The previous section was included to make the point that the Ancient Egyptians were 'black' Africans. This is not to promote 'racial'[6] superiority, but to clear up some misconceptions about who the Ancient Egyptians were. In addition to the history of racial ambiguity that has been perpetuated about the Ancient Egyptians, for the most part, the legacy of the Ancient Egyptians has been tainted by misinformation and misunderstanding.

Ancient Egypt (Kamit) has attained notoriety through biblical stories that tell how the Ancient Egyptians were ruthless and egoistic peoples who enslaved the Jews and had them laboriously build the pyramids and temples of the Ancient Egyptians. Although this has been never been proven through physical evidences, and has been disproven by physical evidences (scientifically disproven), this idea of the Ancient Egyptians holding the Jews against their will and using them to build the pyramids continues to be perpetuated in the Judeo-Christian spiritual texts, traditions, and also through movies other media. Although it has been proven that the pyramids were built by the Ancient Egyptians themselves (the workers' tombs have been found), and not Jewish slaves, the perpetuation of these lies, especially through religion, leads many, including indigenous African people, to repudiate anything Ancient Egyptian, or regard it as a novel ancient mystery or fancy. Ultimately, these falsehoods have served to promote the distancing of Ancient Egypt from the rest of Africa, especially in those parts where the Judeo-Christian influence is heavy.

Another falsity that has been perpetuated that adds to the confusion and misunderstanding about Ancient Egypt and the Ancient Egyptians is the association of Egypt as being located in the Middle East rather than Africa. The promotion of such false information again serves to distance the Ancient Egyptians from other African cultures, nations and peoples and further erodes the legacy of Ancient Egypt as an African nation of great import in the history of African culture and religion. Egypt is clearly located on the African continent.

So, for our studies here, it is necessary to highlight that the wisdom of Ancient Egypt is connected to the wisdom of the rest of African traditions, and did not originate in Asia or any place else, but rather, in Africa, because Kamit (Ancient Egypt) is a major contributor of *African Proverbial Wisdom Teachings*.

Further, since the science of genetics has discovered that all human beings originated in Africa either recently or in the past, before their ancestors migrated to Europe, Asia, and the Americas, it means that all human beings are Africans, and that they therefore should share in the richness, wisdom and benefits of African culture. Therefore, this book is founded in African wisdom and dedicated to all humanity in the hopes that it will lead all human beings to discover the commonality of their experience as personalities with common desires, feelings and rights to dignity, opportunity and fulfillment.

## Colonialism, Imperialism and the Disruption of African Culture and Society

The period of the late 19th century was a time when European countries set out to colonize Africa. This led to the "Scramble for Africa," a period of rapid proliferation of colonies in Africa, established by Europeans. It was mediated by the Berlin Conference (1884 - 1885) where the imperial competitors (European countries) decided how to divide Africa and what constituted a viable colonial claim. This process severely destabilized, and in many cases devastated, and almost completely destroyed, the history, legacy, cultural traditions and social order of African nations. The traditional practice of civilization, social order, religion, etc., were sometimes stopped or completely changed from what they were in favor of the values and traditions of the cultures of the invading European and or Asiatic nations. In some cases, the practice of traditional religion was changed to incorporate western beliefs or it might have been abandoned altogether in favor of a near total adoption of the previously foreign tradition.

Colonialism is the purposeful building of colonies in one territory by people from another territory with the purpose of expanding their [the colonizers'] culture, and acquiring territory, raw materials and other forms of wealth. Colonialism espouses the belief that this is a legitimate and positive endeavor regardless of if there were peoples already in the lands where the colonies are being established. A colony is part of the empire of the home nation and so colonialism is a tactic closely related to the process of imperialism. Colonialism may therefore be regarded as a tool or mechanism by which imperialism is made effective.

Colonialism especially, but not exclusively, refers to a period of history spanning from the 15th to the 20th century when the people from Europe began to build colonies on other continents with accelerated pace and with highly organized logistics and financing. Some colonists wanted to find new commercial opportunities. Others wanted to expand the political power of their nation, while some also wanted to convert the indigenous population by bringing them Christianity [or Islam] and their ideas of civilization [assuming that the colonial powers were civilized]. However, the reality was usually subversion of the indigenous culture, subjugation of indigenous people, displacement of the indigenous peoples and disease or death due to the introduction of harsh slavery and or labor conditions and disease agents against which the natives had no immunities. Most societies on the continent of Africa, experienced varying degrees of detrimental effects, from the disruption of economies and governments, to slavery and the destruction of entire societies through war, famines, disease, colonialism, neocolonialism or globalization. Further, these conditions oftentimes have continued to perpetuate themselves in post-neocolonial times due to the devastating distortion or destruction of the indigenous African culture and society.

Imperialism is the systematic effort of a nation to expand it's power and culture regardless of the desires, feelings or needs of other nations, so that it may, through the subjugation of the peoples of other nations, feed it's insatiable need for wealth, resources, and cheap labor in order to sustain the needs of its own population [especially the elites of the imperial society]. Cecil Rhodes was a prime example of a European imperialist and the imperialist way of thinking.

**Figure 5: Cecil Rhodes: Cape-Cairo railway project.**

Cecil Rhodes founded the De Beers Mining Company and owned the British South Africa Company, which established Rhodesia [now Zimbabwe] for itself. He liked to "paint the map British red," and declared: "all of these stars ... these vast worlds that remain out of reach. If I could, I would annex other planets."[8]

The United States of America constitutes a powerful empire[9] wherein the supposed democratic government does not promote democracy either for its own citizens or the lands the country has occupied [inc. Guam, Puerto Rico, Iraq, Afghanistan, etc.].[10] Throughout the history of the United States of America, as with other imperialist nations, the philosophy of imperialism has been couched in seemingly benign ideals about bringing civilization to other peoples. Invariably, the capitalist market economic system of trade is set up to favor the exploitation of the territories captured by the U.S.A. or other countries coerced by the U.S.A. military or economic forces for the economic benefit and power of the U.S.A. elites and corporations, which pay bribes to the government officials.[11]

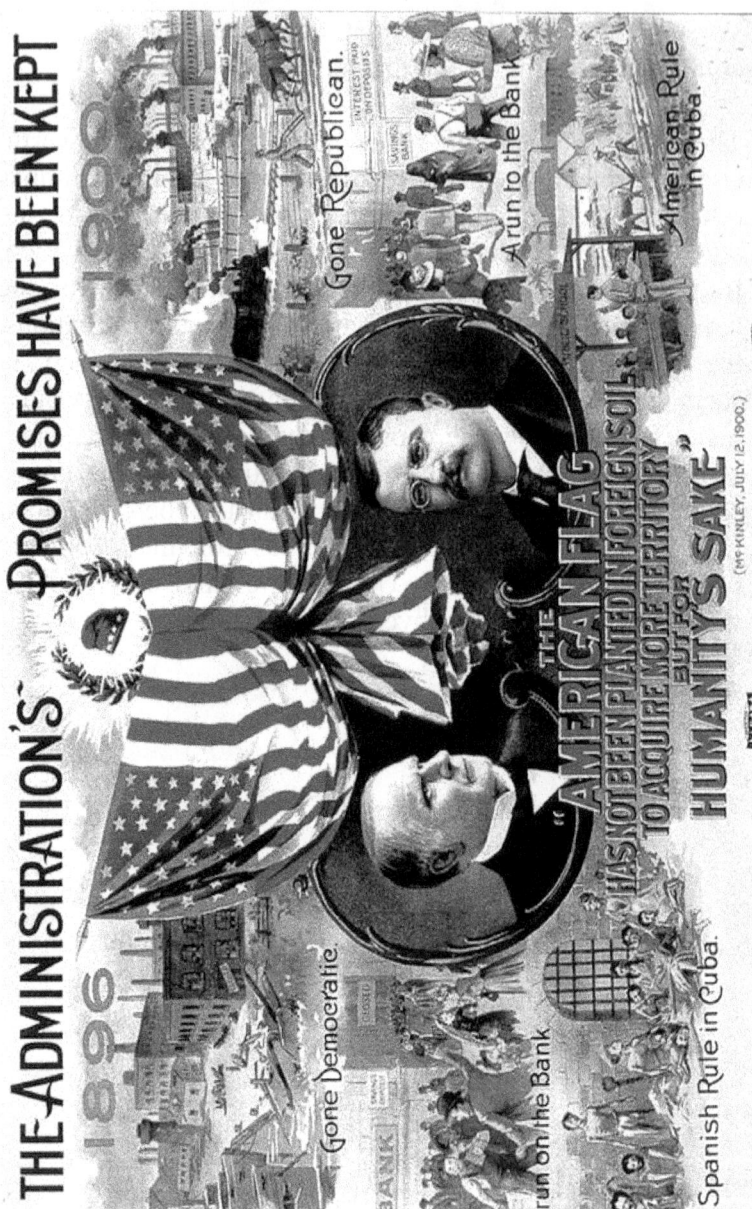

**Figure 6: Year 1900 Campaign poster for the Republican Party. U.S.A. "The American flag has not been planted in foreign soil to acquire more territory but for humanity's sake." -President William McKinley, July 12, 1900.**

The **Scramble for Africa**, also known as the **Race for Africa**, was a most devastating period in African history in which there was a proliferation of conflicting European claims to African territory during the New Imperialism period, between the 1880s and the First World War in 1914. **New Imperialism** refers to the colonial expansion adopted by Europe's powers and, later, Japan and the United States, during the 19th and early 20th centuries; approximately from the end of the Franco-Prussian War to World War I (c. 1870–1914). The period is distinguished by an unprecedented pursuit of what has been termed "empire for empire's sake," aggressive competition for overseas territorial acquisitions and the emergence in some colonizing countries of doctrines of racial superiority which purported to explain the unfitness of "backward" (primitive, less developed and usually non-white) peoples for self-government, and therefore the legitimacy of the imperialist and colonial agenda. The last 20 years of the nineteenth century saw the transition from 'informal imperialism' of control through military influence and economic dominance to that of direct rule.[12] Attempts to mediate imperial competition, such as the Berlin Conference (1884 - 1885) between Britain, France and Germany, failed to establish definitively the competing powers' claims.

The carving up of Africa forced new territorial divisions and language differences among African peoples, which had not previously existed. This process also introduced foreign values that turned some people away from their own indigenous cultural morals and ethics. This process also disrupted longstanding relationships among peoples and separated others from their own kin, later leading to new ethnic conflicts that had not previously existed.

African spirituality encompasses many original forms of religious practice, many of which are related. However, the study of African religion should make a distinction between what constitutes indigenous African religion as opposed to

29

hybrids or extrinsic forms of spirituality due to the special circumstances that were experienced in the African continent. Unlike some other colonial locations, most of the African colonies were exposed to harsh racism and the inhabitants were forced to abandon most customs as well as the indigenous languages. Many village leaders, priests, priestesses, *Griots*[13] and other persons, such as elders, who filled important roles that served to safeguard and carry forward the culture for future generations, were lost in the colonialism and subsequent neo-colonialism periods. So, much of the original indigenous knowledge that was previously passed on orally from generation to generation was also lost. Only that which was written down has been transmitted in an unchanged format.

This is where Ancient Egypt (Kamit) plays an important role. Kamit and Kush (Ancient Ethiopia) were the only pre-colonial African nations that left extensive written records of their culture, civilization and religion. Other nations used the oral tradition, which is more susceptible to interruption or damage due to social disruptions such as war or colonialism. Ancient Egypt (Kamit) left an extensive written record of their activities, philosophy and spiritual culture. The philosophy and spiritual culture of Ancient Egypt had a profound effect on the philosophy and spiritual culture of other African nations as well as some European [especially in Greece] and Asian nations [especially in Mesopotamia and India]; it heavily influenced Judaism and Christianity.

**Figure 7: This ancient Baobab tree in the *Réserve de Bandia*, Sénégal, forms a living mausoleum for the remains of famed local Griots.**

**Figure 8: Senegalese Wolof griot, 1890**

This is significant, because from that record we can derive many aspects of pre-colonial African religion and philosophy. We can then use these to establish the fundamental principles of African religion and philosophy through comparative studies of Ancient Egyptian culture, religion and philosophy with the culture, religion and philosophy of other African peoples.

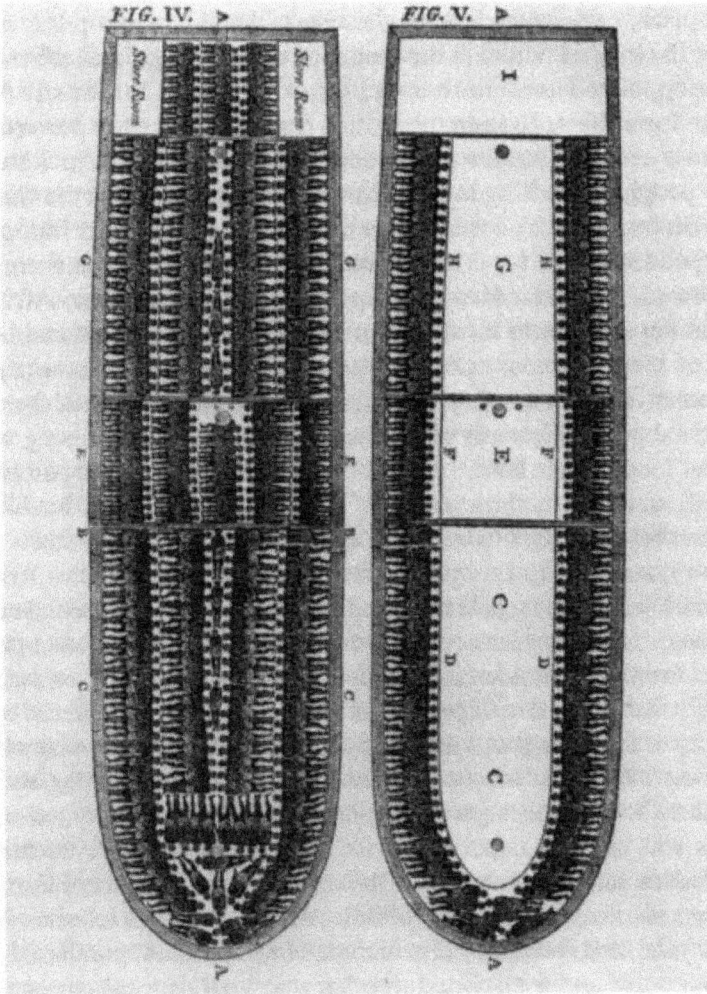

**Figure 9: Diagram of a slave ship from the Atlantic slave trade. From an Abstract of Evidence delivered before a select committee of the House of Commons in 1790 and 1791.**

The transatlantic slave trade led to the physical depletion (depopulation) of human beings on the African continent, whose labor and technological abilities [note the plethora of inventions by African Americans-that benefited the western countries] enriched not the African cultures they were taken from as would have occurred if colonialism had not disrupted the African cultures, but rather benefited the European colonial powers.

**Figure 10: An antislavery medallion of the early 19th century.**

The introduction of foreign religions, customs, and values has had a negative lingering effect, in terms of lower progress, lower development, and slower social, political and economic development generally throughout Africa that continues to be felt to this day.

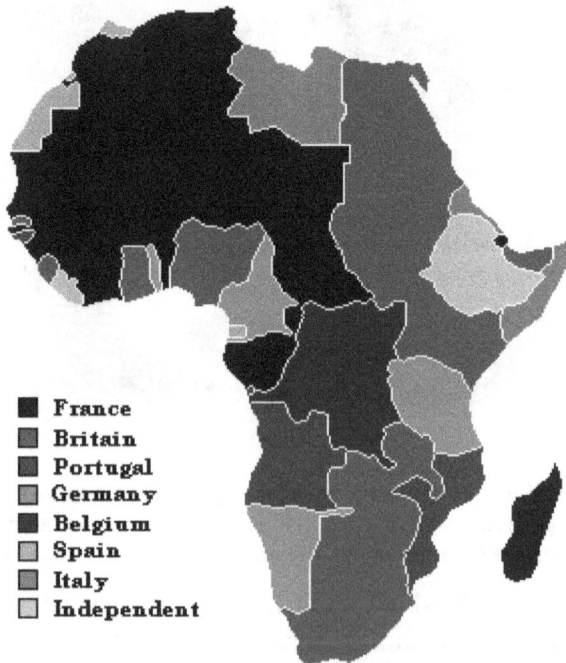

France
Britain
Portugal
Germany
Belgium
Spain
Italy
Independent

**Figure 11:** *European territorial claims on the African continent in 1914*

# African Proverbs and the Methods for The Transmittal of Cultural Knowledge

A frican culture(s) displays three main forms of social transmittal of cultural knowledge, including wisdom teachings, from one generation to the next. The first is the Mythic teaching, the next is through Ritual [and tradition], and the third is through Proverbial Wisdom. The ubiquitous nature of African Proverbs in African societies was described in the following manner.

> In traditional African society, one can hardly hear anyone speak a few sentences without citing a proverb. For the initiated, the citing of proverbs comes naturally without any conscious or special effort. This is as true during ordinary conversation as during formal and solemn discourse. However, proverbs tend to be more purposely cited during serious or formal discourse, such as during proceedings of the council of elders, a chief's court, an arbitration, family meetings, or during exhortations on how to live a morally good life.[14]

The use of proverbs to impart wisdom teaching is an integral aspect of African social education and the transmittal of wisdom to succeeding generations; it is evident throughout the African continent.

prov·erb   Pronunciation [prov-erb][15]
–noun

1. a short popular saying, usually of
unknown and ancient origin, that expresses
effectively some commonplace truth or
useful thought; adage.
2. a wise saying or precept; a didactic
sentence

This volume will focus on *African Proverbial Wisdom Teachings* and their application to ethical practice in leadership and in the basic human relationships of life. It will demonstrate how the foundations of a viable ethical culture and society are present in and can be built and developed with *African Proverbial Wisdom Teachings* without the need for inputs from alien (foreign, i.e., non-indigenous African) cultures and their philosophies. As stated earlier, there are at least three important methods of cultural knowledge transmittal: myths and legend, rituals and traditions, and proverbial wisdom.

Myths and legends impart the story of a people and give a sense of a people's origins and place in the world, the reason for life, its purpose and meaning. Rituals are the means through which the society makes the myth effective, by living the myth in formal religious practice and ordinary life customs and traditions. This process connects the individuals of a population to a shared history and culture, as well as to the common origins of the culture and its legitimacy, and consequently the value it has in time and place among other cultures. Proverbial wisdom is so important and valuable to a people because it contains a storehouse of knowledge about everything from ordinary life situations to advanced spiritual and philosophical wisdom, including ethical conscience and its importance for the successful maintenance of a well-ordered and prosperous society.

**Figure 12: Documented evidences of a relationship in Ancient times between the peoples of Ancient Egypt and those in other parts of Africa**

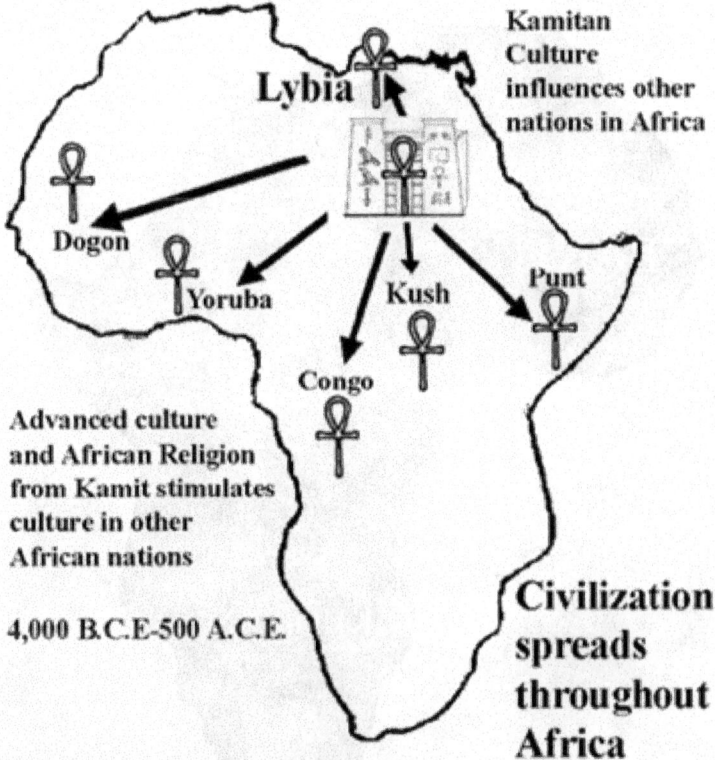

Kamitan Culture influences other nations in Africa

Lybia

Dogon

Yoruba

Kush

Punt

Congo

Advanced culture and African Religion from Kamit stimulates culture in other African nations

4,000 B.C.E-500 A.C.E.

**Civilization spreads throughout Africa**

From the book *African Origins of a Civilization* by Muata Ashby

The developments in Ancient Egypt are central to understanding African Religions and their history, both before and after the rise of Kamitan civilization. This is because there was a close relationship between Neterian [Ancient Egyptian] Religion and other African religions, as there was a relationship between Ancient Egypt and other African nations. The Ancient Egyptian civilization is the oldest Black[16] African society wherein the African Proverbial[17] Wisdom teaching is discernible and extensive. The connections between Ancient Egypt and Nubia, between Ancient Egypt and Ancient Nigeria, and between Ancient Egypt and other African peoples, has been elaborated in several books.[18] Also, the fact that the Ancient Egyptians were "black" Africans and that the original Ancient Egyptians originated in the heart of Africa, the land now called Sudan, has also been documented.[19]

**Figure 13: Major regions of African ethnic groupings**

African spiritual wisdom [non-secular] is closely related to African social wisdom [secular] in such a way that there is hardly a distinction between them in many cases. What is important to understand now is that the fundamental Ancient Egyptian spiritual and social wisdom can be found in other African societies. This means that the principles were a common product of African spirituality from the Bantu regions of West Africa to the Khoisan regions of the south and the Kemetic/Nubian [Nilotic] regions of the North. In this context, Ancient Egypt exemplified the refined principles of African Spirituality and wisdom in a most highly advanced form.

African religion is an integral aspect of African culture and philosophy. It is closely related to African philosophy, especially ethical conscience. However, one of the problems in studying African religion is that most of the cultures, the concepts, traditions and rituals of the varied religions were generally not committed to script form and were only passed down through history in an oral tradition. The exception to this is the Neterian Religion, where there is extensive writing that has survived. This form, (Shetaut Neter {Neterianism} Neterian Religion –Ancient Egyptian Religion) also led to the development of Ancient Greek philosophy and religion, pre-Judaic and Islamic Arabian religions, Judaism, Christianity, Buddhism and Hinduism.[20]

## Egypt In Africa

Some western researchers and or scholars have tried to advance the idea either that the Ancient Egyptian culture and civilization was an independent development or that North-east Africa and Ancient Egyptian culture and religion was part of Middle Eastern (Arabic) culture and religion, and that "Sub-Saharan Africa" is the land of "blacks" who do not have a refined notion of spirituality or philosophy, unlike other peoples of the world that do. From these ideas, negative stereotyping led to the denigration of "Sub-Saharan" African culture and its people as backward savages who live in the "jungle," ignorantly worshiping pagan gods. To those involved in initiating and perpetuating the slave trade, those types of arguments made the enslavement of Africans[21] a more justifiable act during the period of the discovery and colonization of the New World (1492 A.C.E.-1800 A.C.E.), and then the colonization of Africa itself (1750 A.C.E.-1980 A.C.E.). The lack of scriptures or worship in western style churches or Mosques was used by Europeans and Arabs as an excuse to claim that they were bringing religion to Africans, and thus, according to the mandates of their scriptures (especially the Judeo-Christians and Muslims which sanctions the conquering of other peoples to "spread the word"), they were able to justify their actions to themselves as being Divinely inspired and sanctioned. Another problem is that the African religious culture was and continues to be supported by language, oral tradition and shared history.

## The Fragmentation of African Cultures

The introduction of European languages, and the systematic prevention of the large groups of African people from speaking their own native languages or introducing tribal names, has led to the loss of oral memories and histories as well as the introduction of inter-tribal conflicts which were not previously present. This is due to varied socially disruptive changes such as the introduction of distorted *ethnonyms,* names given to the groups of villages or nations by the Europeans based on their anthropological studies and the pre-colonial African names of societies. This means that people who were at one time actually relatives might end up in two or more different, though possibly adjacent, geographic areas, eventually also possibly speaking different languages, and at times even becoming enemies. Due to colonial pressures, their previously common language and common identity was suppressed and diluted, until it's substance was forgotten, leaving only misunderstood rituals or altered traditions as the remnants. Those rituals and traditions could develop into seemingly divergent nexuses for the rise of conflict among people. Then the two begin to see one another as strangers, following the cause of the colonial ruler of one territory against the colonial ruler of the other territory. Thus, the modern interpretation for the word "tribe" as *"a group of people who are descended from common ancestors and ruled by a hereditary "chief," who share a single culture (including, in particular, language and religion), and live in a well-defined geographical region,*[22] is a misapplication as concerns many groups in present day Africa, due to all of the distortion of African society, especially in the past 500 years. Some groups ["tribes"] may have common recent ancestors, but they may not recognize the *pre-ethnic shift* ancestors or ancestral culture [ethnic shift (new language, new religion, political and or economic system)].

In other words, people living in a present day "tribe" may not recognize a connection with common ancestors from among other tribe members, or the tribe may have no such legacy because the disruption by colonists resulted in the tribal memory being lost or in other cases, the members of the tribe may be composed of people who lost their cultural identity (refugees, orphans, etc.) and were brought together for political or economic reasons and forced to speak a different language, etc. This definition of the word "tribe" may be equated with or thought of interchangeably with the term "ethnic group."

However, how can we classify those displaced peoples [Group B], who were originally part of a tribe [Tribe A], whose culture was distorted or transformed, who now speak a different language (perhaps French or English), and who developed a different set of religious beliefs and social traditions, and who were previously part of the African tribe [Tribe A], before the changes? Do we now refer to Group B as Tribe B even though the new group does not have a longstanding history and ancestry of its own? Do we refer to Group B as Culture B even though it came from Culture A [Tribe A] and it now has a distorted Tribe A culture or a product of a synthesis between Tribe A's culture and the culture of those who forced the changes? Lets refer to the culture of those who forced the changes as "Tribe X" (aliens from outside Africa).

How are we to think of any conflicts that may arise between Tribe A and the "new" Tribe B? How should the people of Tribe A and the new Tribe B feel and cope with the conflicts that may arise between Tribe A and the new Tribe B? Are these new conflicts to be thought of as legitimate conflicts between two legitimate "tribes"? Who is responsible for these new conflicts, and how are they to be resolved? Is it best to forget about the original causes for the formation of the new tribe and treat the conflicts themselves? If the causes are not at least acknowledged, would that not lead to new conflicts in the future as well as sustain, legitimize and reinforce the new conflicts? And how are the parties to find peace if the intricacies of their history are not unraveled and the responsible parties are not held responsible? For that matter, what does it mean to hold the "responsible parties" responsible?

## The Absorptive Quality of African Culture

The pragmatic and egalitarian aspects of African cultures, especially when in an environment of less development, social strife or other depressive social, political or economic conditions prevail, promoting less indigenous development, technological and social advancement, have allowed many "alien" [non-indigenous to African] cultural traditions (religious practices, political and economic philosophies, secular interests) to be absorbed into African life. This aspect of African social nature may be referred to as the *Absorptive Quality of African Culture*, which accepts and incorporates many elements from the cultures of other peoples, even non-African peoples. Some of these absorbed cultural elements include, but are not limited to areas such as:

- ✓ Economics
    - o Capitalism
    - o Communism
    - o Etc.
- ✓ Religion
    - o Christianity
    - o Islam
    - o Etc.
- ✓ Social
    - o Consumerism
    - o Secularism
    - o Etc.
- ✓ others

This phenomenon has led to a situation in which many indigenous groups throughout Africa now live with synthesized religions and or social traditions, or completely adopted religions and or social traditions,

42

based on recently introduced [within the last 500 – 1000 years] cultural elements, especially those introduced by peoples from Asia Minor (Arab Muslim conquerors and missionaries) or Europe (Colonists, Christian Missionaries).

Some indigenous groups throughout Africa not only live with or have completely adopted alien (from outside Africa) religions or synthesized religions and or social traditions, but have totally excluded the indigenous traditions of their ancestors and even may repudiate those as pagan (irreligious or hedonistic) or heathen (irreligious, uncultured, or uncivilized). The term *heathen* also refers to unconverted individuals who do not acknowledge the God of the Judeo-Christian Bible; it also refers to a person who is neither a Jew, Christian, nor Muslim.[23] While other religious faiths have been introduced to Africa, such as Hinduism, Buddhism, Baha'i, etc., and some may operate in a more egalitarian fashion[24] than others, still, the idea of the introduction of something new to African culture, regardless of it's compatibility with the preexisting African cultural elements, constitutes a culture changing process that can and has led in some instances to the formation of new cultures (i.e. new "tribes" [new ethnic traditions]), which may lead to new intra-cultural or inter-cultural relationships or conflicts, as well as the possible redirecting of the outlook of African peoples away from local interests, in favor of foreign interests. For example, an African person whose family previously followed an African religion and viewed their wholly land as being located somewhere in Africa may now look to Asia Minor for their "Holy Land," and thus act in ways that benefit that paradigm instead of the previous one, leaving the previous one neglected and deteriorating.

So what are the criteria for assessing if a new cultural development is positive or negative? As this topic relates to African culture in African lands for African peoples, the criteria should be the benefits such new cultural developments may or may not bring in terms of peace, understanding, cooperation, progress and civilization in Africa, and for African people, as opposed to benefiting colonial rulers or the political and or economic interests of other countries. Changes that lead to segregation, discrimination, injustices, conflict, misuse of resources, disruption of people's lives, poverty, denigration, etc., in Africa are to be viewed as negative and undesirable.

African culture has tended to view legacy as a living aspect of life which is passed on from parent to child and from elders and storytellers to the younger generations who grow up and continue the tradition by passing on the myths, culture and religious traditions to the next generation, and so on. It is important to understand that in a normal situation where two viable and longstanding cultures meet, it is unlikely that a substantial number of people from one culture will wholly adopt the cultural elements [language, religion, political and or economic values, etc.] of another culture; that is, unless the culture doing the adoption is somehow deficient, weak or otherwise coerced into doing so. Some methods of inducing the adaptation of cultural elements by people who are currently practicing their own culture are physically preventing them from practicing their culture and forcing them to practice the new culture or by passively preventing them from having any meaningful entry into a social, political or economic order, that they are dependent upon, unless they adopt the language, traditions, religion, etc., that is desired for them. These practices were applied by Arab and later European conquerors and this is in part why today the religions with the largest followings in Africa are not indigenous, but European [Christianity] and Arab [Islam].

## The Oral Tradition Vs. The Written Tradition

The method of transmitting cultural traditions from one generation to the next may be accomplished via recording written texts along with speech [oral] and instruction [teachers], or via speech and instruction alone, orally speaking the history and beliefs and ritual procedures of the cultural tradition. The oral method is called the *Oral Tradition* in African culture, and aside from Ancient Egypt and Nubia, it was the primary method of transmittal of cultural knowledge from ancient times until some African countries adopted foreign script forms (Arabic, English, French, etc.) after being colonized or after their cultures were overwhelmed by hegemonic cultures from the outside. The *Oral Tradition* was passed on through mentorship, rituals, and intensive periods of education, including rites of passage.[25] If such force, as described previously, were applied to cause a people to stop practicing their culture or if the people within the culture who retain the cultural knowledge were unable to pass it on or if their culture should deteriorate for some unknown reason, their method of information transmittal would be also weakened or even impaired. This factor makes the oral tradition more fragile and susceptible to interruption than a written tradition.

What exactly is it that is transferred through the oral or written medium? Firstly, what is transferred is a culture's *Societal Philosophy*,[26] which is also the most important factor influencing the development of a culture. The belief system (and way of thinking) of a culture dictates the culture's worldview and outlook on the purpose and manner in which life is to be led. This also determines whether a culture will develop civilized institutions (that promote life) or institutions that promote destruction, slavery, greed and other vices (that promote Barbarism).

**Table 1: How the Societal Philosophy leads to the cultural outlook**

| Non-secular Dogmatic Philosophy → Secular Philosophy | Spiritual Awareness →or→ Secular Awareness | Culture of Community →or→ Culture of Egoism | →Institutions → | Degrade Life (Barbarism) |
|---|---|---|---|---|
| Non-secular Humanist Philosophy | Spiritual → Awareness | Culture of → Community | →Institutions | Sustain Life (Civilization) |

The Philosophy that a Culture lives by determines the Type of Institutions it creates and if it will become a Civilization or a Barbarian Nation.

✓ A *Societal Philosophy* that recognizes the spiritual connection between all life and the existence of spiritual dimensions beyond the physical world will lead to a culture that develops institutions to promote a spiritual connection to the environment and Creation, humanitarian ethics, justice and protection of nature. This is a civilized culture.

✓ A culture that believes in protecting life and the common good creates institutions that implement that agenda. This is a civilized culture.

✓ The Institutions of a Culture determine its Sustainability.

   o A culture that protects life and the common good is sustainable.

   o A culture that does not protect life or the common good is not sustainable. This is a Barbarian culture.

✓ Civilization is an outgrowth of a well-ordered culture based on a sustainable societal philosophy.

Thus, "Civilization" is an outgrowth of a well-ordered, ethical and spiritually based culture. African cultures generally tend towards positive ethical culture, fairness for both genders, as well as all peoples (including aliens) and a henotheistic/pantheistic spiritual outlook. A culture without a philosophy that affirms universal divinity cannot develop into a "civilization" even if it becomes technologically advanced, because its philosophy will lead to values and practices that deny the universality of human expression as well as the worth and dignity of all human life, thus promoting conflict and negative ethics, i.e. 'Barbarism.' Just as a mother expresses love for a child by taking care of the child, the culture that takes care of people's (not just its own but all people) social needs is a loving and civilized culture. The lack of awareness of a universal and interconnected spiritual basis for all life that occurs in some cultures is due to a disconnect between a society's negative societal philosophy that leads to cultural institutions (manifestations, projections) and lack of understanding of the meaning and purpose of life as an expression of universal existence in which all partake and all are integral. This ideal is a concept that logically means that all should be treated alike and none should be segregated, nor should there be exclusive groups or racial typing, etc.

In traditional African cultures, there is no definite demarcation between the main elements of cultural expression (government, religion, economics, etc.). The lack of a universal outlook[27] in the societal philosophy that a culture is guided by leads to the separation between the secular and non-secular aspects of culture, which leads to intra and inter-cultural conflicts. Internally, the culture develops imbalances with some individuals unrighteously gaining knowledge, power and wealth, while others languish in ignorance, weakness and poverty, being treated with injustice and exploitation. Externally, the unrighteous logic leads to rationalizations of war, and manipulations of other cultures, etc., for the benefit of the unrighteous culture. This leads to social unrest, sufferings among the majority, and animosities and competition instead of cooperation, and disputes that can end in wars in which the poor bear the brunt of the physical, economic and social ills that follow.

## Table 2: The Three Stages of Wisdom Transmittal and the Three Stages of Religion[1]

| The Stages of Social-spiritual Format of Wisdom Transmittal in Traditional (indigenous) African Culture | | |
|---|---|---|
| **Program of Religion (Universal Religion)**<br><br>**3-Stages** | **African Religion** | **Ancietn Egyptian Religion**[28] |
| **Myth (Legends)** | Storytelling (myths – proverbs)<br><br>***Sedjet***<br>"Storytelling, speaking proverbs, sayings of proverbial wisdom" | Listening (to spiritual scriptures, teachings)<br><br>*matnu*-"legend, story, myth" |
| **Ritual (Traditions)** | Ritual (ceremony – Virtuous living)<br><br>*Aru* -"ritual – ceremony" | Reflection (on & practice of the teachings)<br><br>*maut*- "moral of the myth to be remembered." |
| **Mysticism, Metaphysics** | Ecstasy (Transcendental experience)<br><br>*Syh* - "religious ecstasy". | Meditation (on the teachings)<br><br>*uaa* "Meditation" |

---

[1] Ancient Egyptian hieroglyphs are used here because these are the most ancient known African terms for the principles discussed here.

# The Three Stages of Wisdom Transmittal and the Three Stages of Religion

There are three stages or levels of religion, the Myth: *Matnu* 𓈖𓏏𓏤𓅃𓁐 - legend, story, myth, the Ritual: *Aru* 𓇋𓂋𓅱𓅆 - ritual – ceremony, and the *Shetaut Neter* 𓊹𓂝𓐍𓏏𓏤, the mystical. The myth is given through *sdjedt* 𓋴�jedt𓏤 - story telling ( speak proverbs – speak tales). The myth contains *sbait* 𓋴𓃀𓇋𓇋𓏤 spiritual philosophy. In the myth stage the *shemsu.* 𓌞𓋴𓏤, followers of a religion learn about it's story. Then they practice it's 𓇋𓂋𓅱𓅆 *aru* rituals and eventually gain insight into it's mysteries.[29]

So, from an ideal perspective, the complete program and effective practice of religion has three steps which are necessary for the goal of religion, to discover and experience God, as well as one's own immortality. Any spiritual movement that includes these steps can be called "religion" regardless of the name that it may be given by the culture that practices them. These steps include *Myth, Ritual* and *Mysticism* or *Metaphysics*. The table above shows how these three steps or stages manifest in African Religion including Ancient Egyptian written references.

In African Religion, storytelling is a legitimate means of formal education but also achieves the purpose of transmitting myths, which contain the basic concepts of human identity as part of a culture, and offers insight into the nature of the universe and the relationship of the human being and the society with Spirit. So, myths contain a special language of self-knowledge and also proverbs that provide moral education for an ethical society. Rituals are

49

formal (ceremony) and informal (virtuous living) practices which allow a human being to come into harmony within themselves, the environment and the Spirit. This movement leads to an ecstatic experience that transcends time and space and allows a human being to discover and experience the Divine in Creation as well as the realms beyond the physical plane.

## Ethics in Traditional [Pre-Colonial] African Culture and Society

Positive ethics are an expression of the humanity of a society in that they are a manifestation of the conscience of individuals of a society based on their level of spiritual awareness about the interconnectedness between human beings; in other words, the degree to which a human being extends caring and fairness to another human being is directly proportional to the degree of their recognition of the humanity of the other members of society as members of their extended family [one's relatives collectively] and the humane treatment that others should deserve thereby. In African myth, ethics are generally recognized as having divine origins, a moral code given by a divine agency. Therefore, in African philosophy we may refer to ethics (*the rules of conduct recognized in respect to a particular class of human actions or a particular group, culture, etc.*[30]) interchangeably with the idea of morals (*of, pertaining to, or concerned with the principles or rules of right conduct or the distinction between right and wrong; ethical: moral attitudes.*[31]). While in Traditional African Culture, morals or ethics have a divine origin, regarded as instructions from a divine entity, they also relate to natural and practical realities of the physical world, and are not simply arbitrary decrees from an aloof god or goddess. For example, in Ancient Egyptian religion, the goddess Maat

> *A word is (like) an egg.*
> -Sierra Leon proverb

originated right and wrong based on the concept of balance [order] which allows us to recognize an objective universal [cosmic] truth, and therefore, also truth from untruth [wisdom]; here truth is defined as something that is abiding and not what is ephemeral. That pertains to what is true in the physical world as well as the spiritual. Thus, ethical/moral wisdom forms the basis of African Traditional culture and religion and is therefore the foundation of a well-ordered African society.

The foundation of African Proverbial Wisdom is that humanity is originated from the Divine/God,[32] and that humanity is therefore kin or brothers and sisters, which means that there is one humanity, and that alone qualifies every human being to receive humane treatment. If a human being is an expression of the Divine, then it follows that every human being deserves to be treated with civility. Thus, civility is the overarching framework of African Proverbial Wisdom, and civility is the premier expression of humanitarian ethical conscience. This ideal, which can be found in various African traditions, including the Ancient Egyptian, signifies an advanced spiritual philosophical conception of human existence. This is far from the segregating conceptions of orthodox or polarized religious tenets. These tend to place human beings in sectarian clusters or segregated groups based on racial notions or other ideas that separate humanity into illusory segments, as if they were essentially different and apart, having different origins, and thus being somehow composed of different material [genetic material, material elements, etc.]. Part of the ideal of establishing an organization based on these principles is the goal of restoring and maintaining African culture, so that it may bear its particular fruit in the form of physical and non-physical forms of riches, and provide sustenance for its adherents.[33] These conceptualizations have been expressed in the form of *Fundamental African Ethical Axioms* {FAEA} that can be found generally throughout most African societies,

*He who does not cultivate his field, will die of hunger.* - **Ethiopia proverb**

51

demonstrating the greater cultural unity between African societies transcending time, geographical location and language. They also indicate a commonality of ethical thought through developments based on early ancient human discoveries (discoveries by ancient peoples in ancient times) about life, and the continuing interaction and diffusion of African Ethical Philosophy between African societies throughout history.

Thus, in African ethics, the term society relates to all members of the human family. The Ethic of African culture is based on the recognition of fundamental insights about the nature of human existence from a cosmic point of view.

Therefore, African ethics are not based on purely secular ideals, but on principles that are designed to bring order to society for the well-being of all humanity in recognition of three fundamental human/spiritual relationships, the *Triune African Relationships*. For the Baluba peoples of Central Africa, "every person is a "Muntu-wa-Bende-Wa-Mulopo," a "human being from Bende who himself is from God." This statement expresses the *Fundamental African Ethical Axiom* {FAEA} that all human beings are originated or are expressions of God, and are therefore automatically deserving of the respect and care [humane treatment] that is due to all beings that proceed from God.[34]

*Every person is a human being from Bende who himself is from God.* -Baluba proverb [Above: Baluba Mask]

Throughout this discussion of the triune concepts of African socio-spiritual ethics [the *Triune African Relationships*], examples of African Philosophy, from which the ethical teaching is derived, will be included in the form of *African Proverbial Wisdom* statements.

African Proverbs are distilled formulas derived from African ethical teachings, mythic traditions and or ethical wisdom aphorisms that contain the concepts that will be used as references in each teaching that will be discussed. The proverbs or aphorisms represent ideas about ordinary life, but they are also principles of transcendental insight about the nature of existence.[35] Again, it is important to note that in African culture there are no clear demarcations between the secular and non-secular aspects of life. Therefore, the teaching of African Proverbs can relate to religious, economic, government, personal, community, family, and indeed virtually every aspect of life. The African proverbs touch on all aspects of African life especially relating to behavior[36] in areas including: issues of poverty or wealth, health and illness, happiness and sorrow; as well as politics, or commerce, including varied kinds of social endeavors such as: work, building, hunting, farming, fishing, trading, and many others. The proverbs also deal with other activities of society including: sleeping, upbringing, cooking, marriage, walking, healing, childbearing, childrearing, and so forth. There are proverbs that speak on spiritual matters, secular matters, gender issues, sexuality, and many other aspects of human life. The objective of African proverbs is to impart wisdom[37] and morals[38] {positive ethical values} that may be used by a person to confront life and act properly in order to achieve the ultimate goal, which is to create successful relationships of family, society self, and Spirit, that will lead to a successful completion of life's purpose and spiritual evolution.

*A person should not over-indulge in silly habits. - Tonga proverb*

*A proverb is the horse which can carry one swiftly to the discovery of ideas. – Yoruba proverb*

They can be found sometimes in similar forms or in altered forms, in different African societies. Nevertheless, despite the variations, they have a similar formats and intent that affirms the innate value of a human being and the wisdom that, if practiced, allows life to be less troubled and more in tune with nature, community and Spirit. It is fitting that this text should be sprinkled with African proverbs throughout, because these have the effect of a spice of life, giving it meaning. Thus it is said,

> *Proverbs are the palm oil*
> *with which words are eaten.*
>
> -Nigerian Proverb.

It is the intent of the author to allow the proverbs to direct the meaning and tone of the text, which is here only to facilitate the presentation and understanding of the proverbs. We conclude this section with a summary in table form, of the African ethical basis for civilization in the form of three human needs to be met through caring –this is a positive social ethics philosophy worldview or outlook on life [*societal philosophy imperative*].

**Table 3: Blueprint Component of African Society based on Caring for Humanity**

| *African Ethics Wisdom Means is Caring for Humanity* | | |
|---|---|---|
| People (Caring) ↙ ↘ Young + Old | Nature (usage) | Government (social institutions) |
| 3 Basic Needs<br><br>Food<br><br>Shelter<br><br>Opportunity (Career Advancement)<br><br>Self-realization | Purity maintained<br><br>Replenishment Of natural resources | Ethics<br><br>Justice (Social/Economic)<br><br>Meritocracy<br><br>Council of Elders<br><br>Education (Writing, Math) |

**Summary:** Adults are to care for the young and the old as well as nature through ethical government institutions to meet the food, shelter and opportunity needs of all human beings.

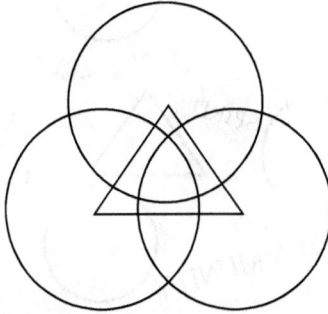

Figure 1a: The Components of Human Existence.

# CHAPTER 1: THE TRIUNE AFRICAN RELATIONSHIPS: AN AFRICAN CONCEPT OF THREE HUMAN RELATIONS

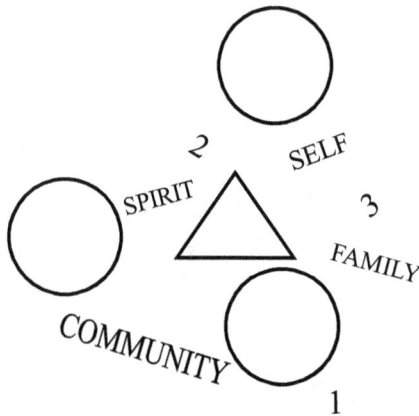

**Figure 14: The Components of Human Existence**

Human existence may defy explanation due to its complexities and seemingly disparate elements that sometimes seem to be in harmony, and at other times seem to be sources of pain, sorrow and insanity. Yet all of the complexities can be reduced to three aspects of existence. If these three aspects were to be understood and properly organized, they would allow for the complexities and complexes of human existence to find order, meaning and a proper place in this world of time and space, and the spiritual worlds.

In African Ethics, it is recognized that a human being is interconnected with the world, with other individuals, and with a subtle cosmic essence that permeates nature and the wider universe. This concept may be considered as another *Fundamental African Ethical Axiom* {FAEA}. There are three important relationships with which every human being needs to be concerned.

The three Fundamental Concepts of African Socio-spiritual Ethics are:

A. **Concept of relationship to family** -The human in relation to the human world.

B. **Concept of relationship to village** - The human in relation to the social world.

C. **Concept of relationship to the universal Spirit** - that expresses as all nature and transcendental of nature - The human in relation to the Spirit ant the spiritual world.

**Figure 15: The Triune Matrix of Human Relations**

The quality of the relationships determines both the quality of life, as well as the outcome, the eschatology of the human journey of life and the fate after death. In reference to the spiritual perspective, some African religious traditions hold an eschatology of dying and becoming a revered ancestor, living forever in the realm of the Supreme Being, while others hold the ideal of becoming one with the Absolute and Transcendental Supreme Being. In any case, the triune ethical foundation for life promotes the desired goal. Thus, a human being works through three dimensions of experience in human life in order to seek fulfillment in life, and after death. These foundations may be thought of as ethical constructs but in actuality, they are also aspects of African Religious practice.

The *Matrix of African Proverbs* may be thought of as wisdom that weaves a pattern of relations, correlations and interdependencies through a triad of elements within and through which the deeper nature of the individual, the higher spiritual self, exists in the world. However, at the same time, it is always intrinsically connected, though perhaps unawares, to Spirit, Family and Community [society, politics, etc.]. If these relations, correlations and interdependencies were properly understood and harmonized, the existence of the self would be fulfilled, and that person would find harmony and peace in life. A society living in accordance with this construct would also discover and maintain social harmony and positive social development. In this construct the self, the inner essence of an individual, is not to be considered as part of the elements of the matrix of Creation. This is because the self, when cultivated through wisdom {the proverbial teaching}, is the aspect of a human being that integrates all of the elements into a harmonious whole. If anything, the individuated aspect of the human being, that which is susceptible to error, foibles, ignorance and is ephemeral, may be considered as an element of the world. The individuated aspect of the human being includes the body, the personality, the ego. However, in this context [cultural relations and the triune wisdom], the individual is part of the family and the self, as an aspect that exists within the individual, at the same time also transcends the world of time and space. In any case, in this paradigm, the ideal to be striven for is self, and not individuality and the egoism of the individual. When this ideal is pursued, the higher self is discovered and the triune elements and their permutations [the myriad of individuals, families, communities, traditions, belief systems, desires, etc.,] find order and harmony, as the individual gives way to the universal, the whole and the true, the higher self. The family and community relations are the foundation for being able to attain the proper relation with Spirit.

**Figure 16: Movement of Human relations from foundation to Spirit.**

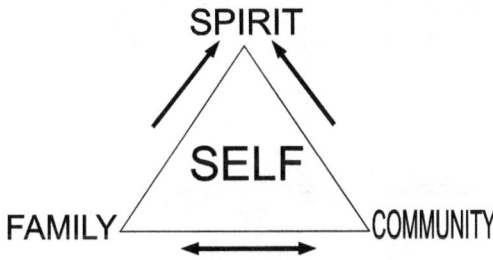

The M*atrix of African Proverbs* may also be conceptualized as a point in the center wherein the individual exists within ever expanding realms of relationships, to Family, Community and God (Spirit). Each layer requires more expansion and with each expansion there is a coming closer to the ultimate reality wherein all relationships are fulfilled.

**Figure 17: The Three Human Relations as Concentric Expanding Circles**

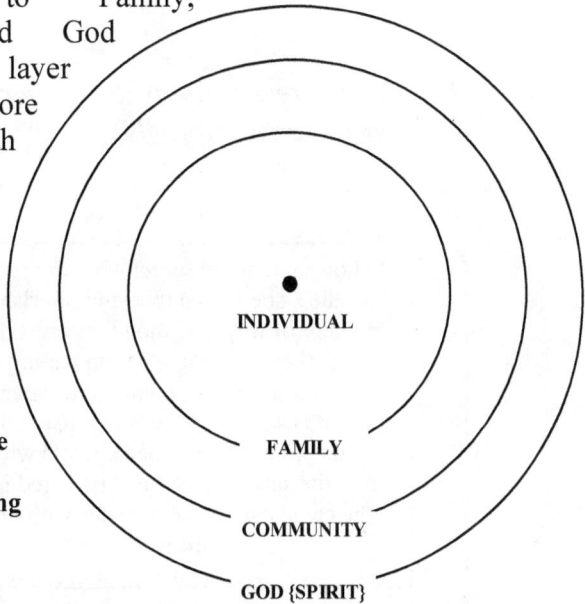

So let's begin by looking at how this triune concept of African spiritual ethics manifests in the Proverbial Wisdom Teachings of Ancient Egypt. The Triune Conceptualizations of African Ethical Philosophy are readily discernible in the following statements contained in the Ancient Egyptian Wisdom Texts. One of the collections of aphorisms that are part of the greater tradition of African Proverbial Wisdom Teachings that may be found throughout African cultures and African History, come from Kamitan/Ancient Egyptian civilization 3,000 B.C.E. to the 21$^{st}$ Century C.E. Some authors refer to this triune concept as a system of religious morals.[41]

## ETHICS OF FAMILY

*(8) Such is, the heated man in his hour. Withdraw from him, leave him alone, The God knows how to answer him. If you Make your life with these (words) in your heart, Your children will observe them.* [42]

*(100) Do not revile one who is older than you, He has seen Ra$^2$ before you;* [43]

"Thou shalt never forget what thy mother has done for thee, she bareth thee and nourished thee in all manner of ways. If thou forgettest her, she might blame thee, she might lift up her arms to God, and God would hear her complaint. After the appointed months she bare thee, she nurseth thee for three years. She brought thee up, and when thou didst enter the school, and was instructed in the writings, she came daily to thy master with bread and beer from her house."
-Ancient Egyptian Proverb

---

$^2$ *The Supreme Being*

## ETHICS OF COMMUNITY (VILLAGE)

*(17) Do not move the markers on the borders of fields, Nor shift the position of the measuring-cord. Do not be greedy for a cubit of land,*

*(18) Nor encroach on the boundaries of a widow. The trodden path worn down by time, He who disguises it in the fields, When he has snared (it) by false oaths,*

*(19) He will be caught by the might of the Moon. Recognize him who does this on earth: He is an oppressor of the weak, A foe bent on destroying your being, The taking of life is in his eye.*

*(20) His house is an enemy to the town, His storage bins will be destroyed; His wealth will be seized from his children's hands, His possessions will be given to another. Beware of destroying the borders of fields,*

*(21) Lest a terror carry you away; One pleases God with the might of the lord. When one discerns the borders of fields. Desire your being to be sound, Beware of Neberdjer, the Lord of All;[44]*

"Know your friends and then you prosper. Don't be mean to your friends. They are like a watered field and greater than any material riches that you may have, for what belongs to one belongs to another. The character of one who is well born should be a profit to him. Good nature is a memorial."
-Ancient Egyptian Proverb

## ETHICS OF SPIRITUAL LIFE

*(3) May you be justified before The God, That a man may say of you even when you are absent, That you punish in accordance [with what is just for the crime]. Good nature allows a man to experience heaven...*[45]

*(14) He who reaches them (God and the Judges of the soul) without having done wrong, Will exist there like a god, Free-striding like the lords forever!*[46]

> *Every human being comes from God –*
> **Baluba of Kasayi in Congo-Kinshasa proverb**

The dimension of family and the dimension of village are phenomenological while the third [spiritual] is abstract and related to that which is beyond ordinary time and space. However, all three areas of human relationship are interconnected through the thread of ethical/moral conduct that gives them structure and viability.

The recognition of the reality of the interconnections between human beings, humans and their social network, and between humans and their spiritual nature, led African clergy, elders and philosophers to the discovery of the triune conceptualizations. They also developed wisdom proverbs, mythic storytelling and religious mythic teachings for greater dissemination of the insights throughout society. These realizations give rise to injunctions about the need for seeing the community as a family, and promoting unity and cooperative actions that will promote collective security and prosperity.[47] Not only is it recognized, in both African Proverbial Wisdom and African Religion, that all human beings proceed from God and are therefore kinfolk who deserve inclusion and caring along with others in the human family, but going further, it is also recognized

> *If relatives help each other, what evil can hurt them?* -
> **Ethiopia proverb**

62

in African religious ethics that a human being is also God, thus deserving the respect and reverence accorded to God Him/Her/Itself. As such the triune relations of human life may be related to the threefold form of Creation instituted by God (Earth, Heavens, Netherworld).

> [Ashanti]
> Supreme God of Heaven, both the sun god and the moon goddess. Nyame created the three realms: the sky, the earth and the netherworld.

> [Ancient Egypt]
> The Ancient Egyptian concept of creation includes three realms. These are the TA, ⟨hieroglyphs⟩ (Earth), Pet, ⟨hieroglyphs⟩ (Heaven ), and the Duat ⟨hieroglyphs⟩ (the Netherworld).

In Ancient Egyptian wisdom, Ta (earth) is the gross physical plane. The Duat (netherworld) is the abode of the gods, goddesses, spirits and souls. Each of these realms are presided over by a member of a great trinity [Ptah (earth), Ra (heavens), Amun (netherworld), which emerge out of the unitary Supreme Being, *Neberdjer*. It is the plane of thoughts, the subtle nature devoid of gross physicality. It is the realm where those who are evil or unrighteous are punished (Hell), but it is also where the righteous live in happiness (Heaven). It is the "other world," the spirit realm. The Duat is also known as Amenta, because it is the realm of Amen (Amun, The Hidden Supreme Being). The Duat is the realm where Ra, the Supreme Being, as symbolized by the sun, traverses after reaching the Western horizon, in other words, the movement of Ra between sunset and sunrise, i.e. at night. Some people thought that the Duat was under the earth since they saw Ra traverse downward and around the earth and emerged in the east, however, this interpretation is the understanding of the uninitiated masses. The esoteric wisdom about the Duat is that it is the

*The human being from Bende who himself is from God—* **Baluba of Kasayi in Congo-Kinshasa proverb**

realm of the unconscious human mind and at the same time, the realm of Cosmic Consciousness or the mind of God. Both the physical universe and the Astral plane, the Duat, are parts of that Cosmic Consciousness.

We may think of the individual as being connected to all the realms of existence, but in need of harmonization through proper relationship to the realms in order to perceive and experience them in fullness. The individual needs to connect first to family and the world of the body and the physical reality; then the individual relates to community [the wider social network and the wider world (including the wondrous expansiveness of the heavens {Astral Plane})]. Then the individual relates to the spirit world[3] [Duat, Netherworld] wherein the soul experiences the spirit nature of Creation and of the inner Self, which are one and the same.

**Figure 18: Baluba Mask**

The idea of seeing existence as a factor of human relationships places the good of humanity at the forefront of social concerns in terms of social planning, economic activities and governmental initiatives. Therefore, African society places higher importance in people's well-being as opposed to the well-being of economic systems, politics or other social activities; or we may say that the human factor is the most important factor in those activities. The basic needs of human beings are more important than the Gross National Product. In other words, African cultural {Proverbial} wisdom would see a society as a failure if the society had high GNP but also poverty, homelessness, citizens without healthcare, destruction of the environment, etc.

---

[3] {composed of subtle energies, inhabited by positive and negative spirit beings, governed by higher order of gods and goddesses, and presided over by the Supreme Being}.

This ancient ideal of traditional concepts of African culture is not unlike the ideals expressed in a concept called Progressive Utilization Theory [PROUT] or the concept of Gross National Happiness. PROUT is a socio-economic theory developed in 1959 by Indian philosopher and spiritual leader Prabhat Rainjan Sarkar (1921-1990). It was conceived as a neo-humanist spiritual philosophy and applied as an alternative global economic model that could eventually replace both communism and capitalism.[50] PROUT strives for 100% employment of those able to work, and the equitable and efficient distribution of resources throughout a society, from the local or "village" community to the larger communities, between communities, and between nations.[51] So, African economics, like PROUT, is not based solely on economic performance, but on results in terms of satisfaction of human needs, and the sustainable usage of raw materials and the environment. Thus, African economics, based on *African Proverbial Wisdom Teachings,* is not based on profit, but on people.

In modern society, economic performance is usually the only way that a society's well-being is measured. However, that depersonalizes the experience of those who are unhappy or unsatisfied with the system. The modern model for determining the health of a society is through measures of national income and output, and not the satisfaction of the basic needs of all members of a society, and their capacity to realize their full potential as human beings.

In economics theory, measures of national income and output estimate the well-being of a society's economy by totaling the value of goods and services produced in the economy. Using a system of national accounting that was developed in the 1940s, the primary measures of national income and output are Gross National Product (GNP), Gross Domestic Product (GDP), Net National Income (NNI), Net National Product (NNP), and Gross National Income (GNI).

*Gross National Happiness* (GNH) is an expression of government and economics in terms of the social quality of life, using more holistic and psychological criteria as opposed to strictly economic criteria such as the Gross National Product. The concept of *Gross National Happiness* was developed in the country Bhutan. Bhutan's King *Jigme Singye Wangchuck* coined the term in 1972 as a response to critics who charged that his economy was growing inadequately. It signaled his commitment to building an economy that would serve the needs of the Bhutanese people first and foremost, as opposed to the economies of most developed countries that follow capitalism and market economic models, that end up providing for the needs of some, while making a minority wealthy, and leaving the rest in poverty. The leaders of Bhutan wanted to focus on Bhutan's cultural and Buddhist spiritual values, as opposed to seeing the management of society in purely monetary, fiscal and material terms, which look at economic growth as the ultimate objective.

This concept recognizes that spiritual and material development complement each other when they occur in balance. Societies that emphasize primarily materialism develop imbalances in the social order and the conscience of their peoples; hedonism becomes strong in such societies. This leads to competition and even war over resources, power and supremacy. Societies that primarily emphasize spiritualism develop orthodoxy, intolerance and religious extremes that lead to religious conflicts, persecutions, backwardness or stagnation in terms of technological development, and even wars.

The system of economics based on African relationships founded in human ethics, such as *Maat* or *Ubuntu,* the *PROUT* ideal of progressive Utilization of social and economic factors for the humanity as a whole, and the Bhutanese ideal of *GNH*, balance for social happiness, are all sustainable ideals and models for creating a beneficial sustainable society that has the potential to develop into a viable civilization.

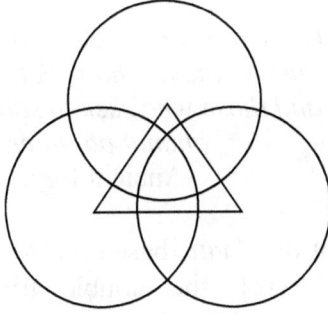

# The Concept of Relative and Absolute Ethics in African Philosophy

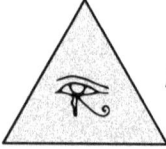

*There are two roads traveled by humankind, those who seek to live MAAT and those who seek to satisfy their animal passions.*
-Ancient Egyptian Proverb

The concept of *Maati* [based on the divinity Maat of Ancient Egypt], the double truth, presents an understanding of two forms of truth, a relative truth and an absolute truth. Therefore, we also derive recognition of two ways of engaging those two truths, either through ethical conduct or through egoistic conduct.[52] In a microcosmic sense, human existence relates to worldly or phenomenological forms of relations. In a macrocosmic sense, the human relates to the universe. In each case, there is an element of commonality, the human being as the agent interacting. Also, there is an underlying principle that runs through the matrix of both micro-existence and macro-existence, a tendency towards balance, a search for fulfilling the innate desire to be fulfilled in both the worldly realm and the spiritual realm, and then finding peace. While in nature, transitory or temporary deviations from balance, order and peace may be observed, the tendency overall, and the ultimate outcome, is towards balance and peace. In music, sound arises from silence, and no matter how loud or intricate the music may become, eventually the sound must inexorably subside and give way to silence. Though we may also notice that the world is ever-changing, that ever-changing-ness of the world (the physical universe, physical realm) may itself be seen as

"There are two roads traveled by humankind, those who seek to live MAAT and those who seek to satisfy their animal passions." –Ancient Egyptian Proverb

another form of constant, but that constant applies to the phenomenal universe, and not to all of the transcendental worlds.

The higher truth behind the apparent changes, activities and movements of the world, in other words, is balance, order, peace and constancy because the changes eventually end in rest; another way to think of it is that even while things are changing, their components do not change and so changelessness is the underlying principle of change. For example, the wood from a tree that was cut down and made into a table continues to be wood either in the form of a tree or a table; so too the constituent elements of Creation remain the same even as they appear to change or even combine to apparently produce different forms. This means therefore that the changeable nature of the world is illusory, conditional, and therefore also not absolute. So we may see and accept changes in nature and in our lives, and at the same time, also notice that there is a constancy aspect within ourselves and within nature itself, even as we seem to see things changing, such as being born, growing up and dying. Throughout those changes that take place in our lives, there is something that does not change, the inner aware self that was the same in youth, adulthood or in old age. In nature, that constancy is seen in the changes of matter from one form to another, but yet not ceasing to exist. For example, a tree can be transformed into a chair, and so the matter that composed the tree remains as the chair. The transient form changes, but the essential nature remains. As it is true in a phenomenological sense, it is also true in a metaphysical sense; the soul of a human being exists in the personality through birth, adulthood, old age and death, and while the body and personality changes, the soul remains the same throughout. But the soul that has identified with the body will develop an egoistic, selfish conscience, and is subject to its experiences.

Ethical life allows a person to discover freedom from the transient nature of life and Creation; it brings him/her to harmony with life, family, community and with the spirit world. In that harmony a person can be free to leave the world behind while alive and thus live in peace; and then, at the time of death, that person is able to move freely to take a rightful place in the afterlife. Therefore, ethical experiences will lead to a positive movement towards successful relations with family, community and spirit. Unethical experiences lead to negative movement away from successful relations with family, community and spirit, leading to suffering while alive, and then also after death.

From a practical standpoint, a society should be interested in promoting ethical conscience, because that in turn fosters conditions that are conducive to successful relations with family, community and spirit. However, that interest is not just because ethics promote peace and order, but because that peace and order allows a higher process to occur, the spiritual evolution of the individuals and society as a whole, which cannot take place if the society is in a state of perpetual or frequent social chaos.

Occasional deviations from order and peace do occur in nature and these do play a part in the overall evolutionary scheme of existence. Sometimes a deviation from the path that a person or society is on is necessary to promote certain awareness of changes needed to move forwards.[53]

> *Smooth seas do not*
> *make skillful sailors.*
> **-African Proverb**

However, these periods are temporary and are not the mainstay of existence. Therefore, they cannot be considered as underlying realities of existence; the tendency is always to return to the balance, the peace. Using the metaphor of music again, just as the sound of music has a beginning, at some point it must end, and silence must inevitably return. That silence is the higher underlying reality and the music is the ephemeral aspect. Though the music may assist the person playing or listening to it to feel or understand something about life, it in itself is transitory and therefore only a relative reality. The persons that have learned something move on and grow. Growing is learning to discover the transcendental aspect, the constant aspect of life, and that is the highest ethic. Discovering the transcendental aspect of life allows one to move away permanently from pettiness, egoism, ignorance and the vices of the personality that lead to egoistic[55] desires and thoughts, which produce pain and sorrow in life. Egoistic desires and thoughts refer to those based on selfishness and ignorance about the higher realities of the soul and that which is transcendent.

> *As the wound inflames the finger,*
> *so thought inflames the mind.*
> **- Galla Proverb**

Those desires and thoughts of understanding, when developed, tend away from violation of the ethical standard and are the pathway towards successful relations in family, society and spirit. A society that does not promote higher knowledge[56] will ultimately fail to produce conditions of optimal relations.

> *Knowledge is like a garden:*
> *if it is not cultivated,*
> *it cannot be harvested.*
> **-Cameroon**

> *One must talk little, and listen much.*
> **-Galla Ethiopia proverb**

So, in a society where a person or culture engages in too much talking[57] and too much activity,[58] it can move the personalities away from the constant of the universe which is more akin to silence and listening, and those personalities can lose the insight of the transcendental constancy underlying life, and thus lose the way in relations of family, society and spirit.[59]

> Clothes put on while running come off while running. -
> **Ethiopia proverb**

So the underlying essential nature of existence is unchanging, immortal, eternal spirit. That spirit permeates all things in the phenomenal world. Through proper ethical conduct, which creates a space for proper relationships, a human being can discover peace and harmony in life, and also that unchanging, immortal, eternal spirit, and so also realize his/her own unchanging, immortal, eternal nature.[60]

> He who is free of faults, will never die.
>
> -**Buganda Uganda proverb**

Ethical living allows sensitivity and awareness of the higher reality to occur, while chaos, disorder, violence, disharmony, etc., do not allow the higher realization to occur.[62]

> Those who live today will die tomorrow, those who die tomorrow will be born again; Those who live MAAT will not die.
> -**Ancient Egyptian Proverb**

Occasional disharmony is a normal occurrence because the personalities of most human beings are in constant flux, and not firmly tied to an ethical foundation or based in emotional stability, due to egoism. The society itself, not being based on a firm ethical foundation, may promote conflicts for example, due to the unethical, unequal distribution of resources.[63]

> Two *buttocks*
> *do not fail to make a friction*
> – **Tonga Proverb**

Often, the conflicts need not be engaged or confronted actively but passively, with understanding, compassion and silence.[64]

> *If you meet a disputant who is not your equal or*
> *match, do not attack, they are weak.*
> *They will confound themselves.*
> *Do not answer the evil speech*
> *and give in to your animal passion for combat*
> *by venting your self against them.*
> *You will beat them through the reproof of the*
> *witnesses who will agree with you.*
> *–**Ancient Egyptian Proverb***

> *Familiarity breeds contempt; distance breeds respect.*
>
> **- Nigeria proverb**

However, the normal, ordinary, minor forms of disharmony that occur in day to day life are to be expected and have their own lessons to teach in relation to patience, tolerance, forbearance, and so on. These may be engaged by restoring balance and order, which may simply require temporary separation and rest.[65] In more severe cases, it may require the restoration of equitable human rights, which may have eroded over time or due to some social disruption.

Though chaos is not an absolute reality, it has some beneficial effects as described above, but only as long as it is not a constant and perpetually disruptive element in human life. In most cases, temporary disruptions [minor chaos] can be ignored, and they dissipate[66] on their own. For minor infractions this is the preferred manner of engagement {non-engagement}; this is the passive approach. In other cases, chaos may need to be

> *It takes two to make a quarrel.*
>
> **Ashanti Ghana proverb**

engaged {confronted} actively. Verbal and physical violence are extreme forms of chaos that often destroy both parties engaging in the conflict by leaving many seeds of future chaos in the form of resentments, prejudices, hatreds, and grudges. In a person's life they may need to violently expel a poison in order to reestablish balance and health in the body that was lost due to an original incorrect act, eating the bad food, deviating from the ethics of eating fresh and nutritious food. In the same way, it is possible to encounter instances in life where violence is needed to rectify an injurious situation in order to return to balance and health.

What is the ethical use of violence? A person may need to violently prevent another person's injury by shoving them out of the path of an oncoming vehicle. A person may need to strike an attacker in order to prevent injury to themselves or someone else. However, the ethical use of violence means engagement for self-protection {self-defense} and not for egoistic desires that are unrighteous. In this case, egoistic desires refer to attacking others out of fear, greed, sadism, ignorance, etc. In the same way, in order to counter the incorrect movement that led to an unbalanced situation, a society may need to have temporary upheaval in order to create conditions that are conducive to a return towards balance and peace. However, the higher goal would be to avoid the need for that in the first place, by working to promote balance, justice and opportunity in the society.

In a practical sense a court case may be seen as a deviation from a balance as, for example, where two neighbors were living in peace until one decided to build a fence over another's land either by accident or on purpose. The ethical violation is a deviation from order, balance and peace and the court case presided over by a judge may be seen as another form of deviation that is designed to produce a return to balance and peace by rendering a just verdict.[67]

*A little subtleness is better than a lot of force.* - Zaire – **The Congo proverb**

74

> *Go not in and out of court that thy name may not stink.*
>
> *Punish firmly and chastise soundly,*
> *then repression of crime becomes an example.*
> *But punishment except for crime*
> *will turn the complainer into an enemy.*
>
> **–Ancient Egyptian Proverbs**

It would be impossible to fashion a society where unethical behavior is absolutely absent, because human beings are complex, containing seeds of past life ignorance or present misunderstanding.[68]

Also, because deviations begin in subtle[69] ways, not noticed until they take on active characteristics, it is

*Evil enters like a needle and spreads like an oak tree.*
*-Ashanti Ghana*

possible to create a foundation and structure for society wherein the deviations from ethics can be confronted constructively, and the violators can be led to understand the error and repair the breach, thus creating the conditions for a growing and evolving culture that moves towards positive development and enlightenment. Just as negativity can come into a society in subtle ways, so too, the countering force of truth and righteousness can be implemented in subtle but powerful ways.[70] This is especially important when developing institutions that educate young people; this is why great care should be taken in childrearing.[71]

*A little subtleness is better than a lot of force.*
*- Zaire – Congo proverb*

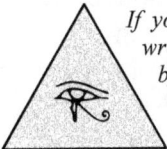

> *If your child accepts your words then no plan of theirs will go wrong. So teach your son to be a hearer, one who will be valued by the officials, one who will guide their speech by what they have been told, one who is regarded as a hearer. The children will reach old age if they listen to the wise words of their parents.*

*If you are wise, train children to be pleasing to God. If they are straight and take after you, take good care of them. Do everything that is good for them. They are your children, your KA begot them. Don't withdraw your heart from them. But an offspring can make trouble. If they stray and neglect your council*

75

*and disobey all that is said, with mouth spouting evil speech, then punish them for all their talk.*

–Ancient Egyptian Proverbs

Every society requires a foundation (societal philosophy of life) and structure (cultural institutions that support its societal philosophy)[72] in order to successfully allow its members to survive and develop. It should be noted that a society can function for a time without an ethical foundation, but it must have some kind of foundation. Yet, the ethical foundation which leads to true civilization is more viable than the unethical foundation which leads to barbarism, because it is based on natural truths that are automatically sustainable. In the culture with the ethical foundation, there will be a tendency towards equitable and sustainable use and distribution of resources while in the culture with the unethical societal philosophy, the tendency would be more towards over-consumption, injustice, accumulation of power and wealth by minorities, and tyranny.

> *"If you don't stand for something, you will fall for something."*
> - African Proverb

If a society is lacking in its foundation and structure, its members will lack direction and purpose. This can lead to deviations from the ethical standard, and violations of the universal laws of nature.[73] The underpinning for a society with an ethical societal philosophy is the realization of the underlying filial, social and spiritual communion of the human family, which promotes caring for all. Then the structure of the society organizes cooperation in peace and order, which provides the necessities of life {food, water, shelter}, and the equitable distribution of resources[74] for the benefit of all. After that, the institutions of the society need to promote the ideal and opportunity for the self-actualization[75] of the individuals in terms of their being able to

> *Mutual affection gives each his share.*
> -Galla Ethiopia proverb

fulfill their roles in their families and society, to develop their skills and become valued contributing members. This includes a mechanism for redeeming those who have deviated from the ethical standard set by society, which are themselves reflections[4] of the ethics in nature. Such a social construct will also allow the opportunity for its members to grow spiritually, to discover the higher nature of reality. So, the ideal African vision of self-actualization is one in which a human being discovers both worldly fulfillment and spiritual enlightenment.[76]

> "Men and women are to become God-like through a life of virtue and the cultivation of the spirit through scientific knowledge, practice and bodily discipline."
> —Ancient Egyptian Proverb

Another integral component of ethics in African philosophy is the aspect of cause and effect. The ethical act leads to order and truth, and this produces harmony and joy. The unethical act leads to a deviation from order and truth, and the deviation produces suffering and pain. This affects the individuals as well as the society.[77]

> The African race is like an Indian rubber ball, the harder you dash it to the ground the higher it will rise.
> – Bantu (African Proverbs by Gerd de Ley)

The goal of life is the perfection of virtue such that one's actions lead to one's successful fulfillment of the responsibilities of life, and the successful entry into a transcendental life. This also means fulfillment of the relationships of life, and after the physical existence, to become an honored ancestor who has fruitfully taken the

---

[4] The standards of ethical principles set by society are reflections of the principles of balance and order embedded in nature.

rightful place in the spirit world. This also means discovery the nature of Spirit, thus in other words, self-mastery in life and self-knowledge, enlightenment and divinity, after death. Ancient Egypt, being the oldest known and literary society of Africa, recorded the ethical *Maat* philosophy in a text known as the *Pert m Heru*, commonly referred to as the "Book of the Dead". Maat relates to truth, order, and balance. The main concepts of Maat Philosophy of Ancient Egypt were listed in a compilation referred to as "The 42 Precepts of Maat".[78] The fruition of a life lived by the ethical/moral code was recorded in papyri and inscriptions on the tombs of those who professed success in the ethical life; the statements or declarations of ethical/moral conduct reflect similar concepts also found elsewhere throughout Africa.

Thus, necessarily, African Ethics relate to duties and responsibilities in each of the triune areas, family, village (community), and spirit. The purpose of this is to promote the optimal conditions in each area, and prevent the deterioration of them, in order to foster harmony in the family, community (including the environment), and with the spirit world So, the African Ethic is proactive in presenting regulations for fostering harmony and reactive in addressing violations of the regulations in order to restore harmony. Because there are three areas of moral ethic, there are three corresponding regulations that a human being must observe and uphold in order to maintain balance and harmony in each area of moral responsibility. Doing so will eventually lead to the fulfillment of one's life.

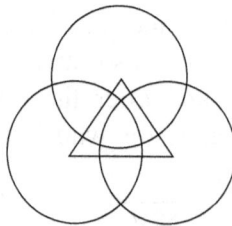

79

# Falsehood and the Degradation of Society

> *One falsehood spoils a thousand truths.*
> -Ashanti of Ghana

A human being has three modes of action: thought, word and deed. Actions can be legislated, but opinions cannot. Thoughts can be manipulated and influenced, in some cases, through social influences, appeals, deterrents or incentives. However, they are most affected by the immersion in the societal philosophy practiced most widely and inculcated through childhood rearing and education. Thoughts can be influenced by subtle energies of the universe and from other beings (human and non-human); in the individual personality they are formed by a combination of innate psychological and spiritual aspects of the personality, combined with upbringing. Both negative and positive influences can affect the personality. Negative thoughts and feelings can be fostered in the personality through negative influences during rearing and education, i.e., a dysfunctional upbringing. Positive thoughts {ethical} may be promoted, if not instilled, by upbringing and counseling based on positive {beneficial to society} societal values applied to all members of the society. For a society desirous of developing an ethical and sustainable civilization, this means providing a proper environment that is conducive to the ethical development of human beings. This includes having proper role models who can teach African ethical wisdom by word {lecture} and by example {deed}. Actions may be controlled by influencing the development of empathy, sympathy and compassion, as well as wisdom about the interconnectedness of life. Next, the society can implement regulations of the socially acceptable speech and the socially acceptable actions.

> *A cutting word is worse than a bowstring; a cut may heal, but the cut of the tongue does not.*
> **- Mauritania proverb**

In reference to speech, great care to cultivate positive speech is required in order to maintain and promote the harmony of speech, since in some cases, the wrong kind of speech (words, ideas, feelings expressed, intent, etc.) can do more harm than physical violence.[80]

> *Put a bridle on thy tongue; set a guard before thy lips, lest the words of thine own mouth destroy thy peace On much speaking cometh repentance, but in silence is safety.*
> **- Ancient Egyptian proverb**

There is an ancient Egyptian word for lie and the hieroglyphic text reveals the deeper implications of how lies and disingenuous speech can bring down a society. The Kemetic (Ancient Egyptian) term *kz* — "lie – deceive" contains the hieroglyph which means wall. When the glyph is placed on its side, it signifies a falling wall, which means the fall of the protections of a city, and thus the downfall of the village itself. Thusly, the ruination, the downfall of society, can be found when the societal philosophy is governed by dishonesty, mendacity, and falsehood.[81]

> (41) *Do not speak falsely to a man, The God, abhors it; Do not sever your heart from your tongue, That all your strivings may succeed. You will be weighty before the others, And secure in the hand of The God. God hates the falsifier of words, He greatly abhors the dissembler...*
> THE INSTRUCTION OF AMENEMOPE –Ancient Egyptian Wisdom Texts

Falsehood leads to lack of trust[82] and negative feelings, resentments and negative actions that harm families and society.[83]

> *Where trust breaks down, peace breaks down.* -**African Proverb**

> *Truth keeps the hand cleaner than soap.*
> –**Nigerian proverb**

> *One falsehood spoils a thousand truths.* -**Kenya proverb**

The forms of speech that promote most disharmony, disunity, conflict, anger, hatred, greed, etc., begin with falsehoods, and develop to unrighteous egoistic desires, culminating in violations of the ethical code. These are to be discouraged, if not prevented, as these promote ethical decay in individuals and reduced capacity of the village to maintain the truthful pursuit of the fulfillment of the Fundamental Concepts of African Socio-spiritual Ethics, the harmonious and successful attainment and realization of family, village (community), and spirit relationships.[85] Falsehood should not be thought of only as lies told between people, but of untruths that a person may believe about the world, the universe, spirit, and him/herself.

> *"Don't repeat slander nor should you even listen to it. It is the spouting of the hot bellied. Just report a thing that has been observed, not something that has been heard secondhand. If it is something negligible, don't even say anything. He who is standing before you will recognize your worth."*
> —Ancient Egyptian Proverb

Seemingly harmless words can produce great unintended negative consequences.[86] Therefore, speech that is characterized by purposeful disingenuousness, falsehood (lies), invention, untruth, slander,[87] dishonesty, etc., is to be considered as the highest violation of the ethical code, and should be dealt with in a timely manner and decisively.[88] Other forms of speech such as error, misunderstanding, etc., are to be treated with understanding, and counseling through discussion and revealing facts, and assigning the proper action to redress imbalances caused by the error.

> *Great events may stem from words of no importance*
> **-Kenya proverb**

> *The end of a lie is grief.*
> -Nigeria proverb

In reference to physical actions, things done with the body, errors or accidents that result in the injury of others are to be treated with counseling as above. Violence can manifest as hurtful words or threats,[89] actions that are intended to hurt others, or omission of action that could help others. Physical violence is to be considered as the advanced development of false negative thoughts of one's desires, which one has perceived to be realities that will bring personal happiness, even at the expense of others. This is in contrast to seeing happiness as inner fulfillment and seeking the happiness of others by serving/assisting them, and making sure they have their needs for life provided for, which leads to peace and harmony.[90]

> *Happiness is openness to all people.*
> –African proverb

The pursuit of one's own desires at the expense of others leads to negative feelings, speech and physical action in violation of the ethical code; so negative desires are a cause of violence that need to be addressed by a society and its values, but physical violence should be seen as an outcome of a process wherein negative ethic has developed in an individual or a society. Therefore, in this area, society has failed to lead the individual(s) to a harmonious and peaceful, balanced condition, and consequently the individual or sub-group is not the only responsible party for the breakdown in the practice of the ethical code. Thus, the society, as well as the individual violators of the code, need to be mended in order to bring the society to a condition wherein the error that led to the violation is resolved and the issues that arose from the violation are also resolved. Nevertheless, physical violence should be dealt with in a timely manner, and decisively. Actions with purposeful intent to harm others are discussed below.

The idea of making a distinction between error and purposeful intent recognizes that human action flows from thought to word[91] and deed. If the thought arises from ignorant desires, lack of knowledge[92] or misunderstanding, though the outcome of the action may be the same as if the negative deed was performed with conscious intent, the ethical cause is not the same, and therefore they should be treated appropriately[93] instead of trying to assign one solution for all problems.

> *When the heart overflows, it comes out through the mouth.*
> **– Ethiopia proverb**

> *He who does not know is forgiven by God.*
> **–Swahili proverb**

> *A wise man who knows proverbs can reconcile difficulties.*
> **-Niger proverb**

> *The heart of the wise man lies quiet like limpid water.*
> **- Buganda proverb**

The idea of maintaining an ethical code for society is not only to mete out punishment for a given violation, but also to seek to heal a wound or discrepancy that caused the imbalance that led to the infraction in the first place, and thereby restore and protect the integrity of the family and community of a healthy, vibrant and strong nation.[94] Punishment, except for cause, may be thought of as egoistic, for the purpose of exerting power over others, the sadistic pleasure of seeing others suffer, or for the purpose of unrighteous gains such as power and wealth, etc.[95]

*The ruin of a nation begins in the homes of its people.*
-Nigeria proverb
Ashanti proverb of Ghana

> *"Punish firmly and chastise soundly, then repression of crime becomes an example. But punishment except for crime will turn the complainer into an enemy."*
> —**Ancient Egyptian Proverb**

If a society lacks in wisdom, in the dispensation of resources and justice, it will end up in a condition wherein it may have law and order, but without justice[96] or fairness.

> *The one who has wealth at home will not be partial,*
> *He is a just man who lacks nothing.*
> *The poor man does not speak justly,*
> *Not righteous is one who says, "I wish I had...*
> - **Ancient Egyptian proverb**

Therefore it becomes a tyranny, usually of the dominant group. This foments discontent and a rebellious nature[98] and requires the dominant group to use police or military power to maintain control and impose their will on the population.

> *When free men are given land, They work for you like a single team; No rebel will arise among them...*
> -Ancient Egyptian proverb

Bi-nka-bi. Obi nka obi (bite not one another). Avoid conflicts.
Symbol of Unity, peace, harmony

[Ashanti mythology and adinkra symbols]

# CHAPTER 2: ETHICS FOR LEADERSHIP ACCORDING TO AFRICAN PROVERBIAL PHILOSOPHY

> *Good behaviour must come from the top.*
> -South African Proverb

100

# What is Ethics?

## Ethics or Morality

What should be the basis of ethics for those who want to assume leadership positions in a society based on *African Proverbial Wisdom Teachings*? Which kind of ethics or morality should guide the society and be upheld by its leaders? In the study of philosophy and proverbial wisdom teachings, it is important to distinguish between morality and ethics for the purpose of understanding the distinctions as applied in scholarly studies, and their proper application in leadership roles.

Ethics may be defined[101] as: A set of principles of right conduct; theory or a system of moral values: "An ethic of service is at war with a craving for gain" (Gregg Easterbrook); **ethics** *(used with a sing. or pl. verb):* The

85

rules or standards governing the conduct of a person or the members of a profession: *medical ethics.*

Ethics here is to be thought of as a system or way of thought arrived at through the reasoning faculty of the mind. It is a framework for balanced and equitable human relations developed through logical and rational, and perhaps scientific, reflections based on experiences gained from the world of human interactions. When thought of as a discipline separate from religion, ethics has been associated with reason, science, humanism or secular humanism.

> Kurt Vonnegut, Honorary President of the AHA [American Humanist Association],[102] said: "*being a Humanist means trying to behave decently without expectation of rewards or punishment after you are dead.*"
> The AHA's more complete definition from its website is as follows: "*Humanism is a progressive lifestance that, without supernaturalism, affirms our ability and responsibility to lead ethical lives of personal fulfillment that aspire to the greater good of humanity.*"

## Ethics in Religion: Views and Approaches

Morality {ethics}, in religion, is arrived at through divine agency or enlightened leadership, but this does not preclude a philosophical or phenomenological reflective process. In religion, ethics are also referred to as morals or a system of morality that is enjoined to promote virtue. Virtue is promoted to purify the personality and cause it to become a proper vessel for higher spiritual experiences. So in religion, rules or regulations for proper conduct may be given to religious aspirants/practitioners by a god or goddess, or by a personality that has or has had communion with the Divine directly, or with a god or goddess. Examples of divine agency are plentiful. In Ancient Egyptian religion, it is held that the Laws of Maat were given to the priests and priestesses by the god Djehuty. In

Judeo-Christian religions, it is believed that Moses received the Ten Commandments from God. So when thought of as a discipline within or arising from religious experience, ethics has been associated by theologians with morality. In this context, morality may be defined as "a concern with the distinction between good and evil or right and wrong; right or good conduct 2: motivation based on ideas of right and wrong.[103] In the book, *Godless Morality: Keeping Religion Out of Ethics*, Bishop Holloway provides an argument to develop a non-theocentric ethic for the new millennium. Another ethicist, Joseph Fletcher, also provided a strong argument using the concept of situational ethic.

Such a moral system as described here [African Ethics based on African Proverbial Wisdom] requires the consent of those who use it based on persuading them as to its validity due to its logic and wisdom, as opposed to a system that is imposed, and simply to be obeyed or an autonomous and self-imposed system based on the goodwill or self interest of individuals. Thus, this kind of ethical system [African Ethics based on African Proverbial Wisdom] potentially undermines the absolute authority of the Church, Synagogue, Mosque or Temple, and even the State [if the state government is based on self-interest, greed, partisanship as opposed to logic and wisdom] because it is based on universal and altruistic cosmic (natural) principles) which benefit all and not particular groups, or institutions. Most powerful social institutions have granted themselves the power as the preeminent ethical or moral authority, often by invoking divine authority or through fear, in other words, the wrath of God, eternal damnation, and the like while not seeking to determine the universal principles of ethics and applying these universally (including themselves). There are many people who have become disappointed with organized religions due to the contradictions they have engendered over the years, as well as the conflicts in society and between nations that they have fomented.

The secular form of government appeals to many who reject the authoritarian state model of laws which frequently are broken, even by the state itself [corrupt politicians and other leaders of society as well as bureaucrats who receive their favors]. Of course the state is composed of people, and some unethical people seek to follow the letter of the law, even though it may be transcending the bounds of what is moral. That boundary, having been crossed, leads to the degradation of culture (due to the deterioration of trust in the government and the resentments that are engendered), producing litigious societies and disappointment with the legal system.

Nevertheless, many people have come to feel that the current society wherein the Bible or some other scripturally based ethical system is no longer sought after as a source of ethical and moral wisdom is insufficient. Yet, many people move away from religious based moralistic forms of social organization because they feel it has been abused by unethical religious leaders or it may be seen as too inflexible to meet the needs of modern society. While there are many people who surrender themselves and give blind obedience to religious [church or other religious based organizations] or state authorities, there are many who prefer to live a "spiritual" life, referencing themselves to the religion, but not to the church, mosque, synagogue or temple. They may consider themselves as "Christians", or "Muslims" or "Jews", etc. but do not regularly or ever attend the Church, Synagogue, Mosque or Temple. A society that is governed by blind allegiance to divine authority or to those who profess to be guided by divine agency is not necessarily the same as a society governed by universal ethical principles. While universal ethical principles may be derived from a divine agency it is not guaranteed that the leaders of such a society (theocratic) will adhere to those principles and not follow more self-serving policies.

In the book, *The Evolution of Morality and Religion,* by Donald M. Broom, the author argues that morality and the central tenets of religion are valuable. Yet, he advances the idea that morality is founded in biology, and as such, has evolved with human biology. According to this paradigm, human ethics have developed due to natural selection. He also holds that religions are therefore to be considered as the structures sustaining morality. Thus, he holds that morality is an effect of the biological processes undergone by human beings, in this case evolution. From this vantage point, the accepted codes of conduct that religions have instituted may be seen as features of the human societies that developed throughout the history of the world because it was beneficial and in evolutionary science. In terms of evolution and natural selection, the idea is, what is beneficial is desirable and retained, and what is not beneficial is undesirable and lost. In other words, if morally acceptable behavior does benefit humans and animals, then that behavior will be seen as desirable simply from a practical point of view. Then, the purpose of religion would be to support and encourage those behaviors that are desirable.

If the aforesaid is true, then ethics would be considered as a 'secretion' of the human personality. There would be no recognition of an all-encompassing ethical matrix of life that includes human existence, as well as nature and the universe. Ethics, then, is internal to the human, and not external. However, how do we explain the fact of human beings who have acted in contradiction to their personal desires in order to uphold ethical principles that are detrimental to themselves? For example, in a certain legal case, a person's telling the truth will lead to their loss of property. Yet we know that people lie, and a person of different character could have lied and retained their property. If the moral imperative for a society is an expression of the personality, an effect of the biological processes, why was it contradicted? If we consider the situation above with a person who told the truth but lost their property as being a loss for an individual, but a gain for the society (because that person made an ethical environment for society), what about the liar? How does a liar affect the ethical condition of the society? The liar's personal desires clouded her/his ethical conscience, but that is not the answer to the problem, the question of the source of ethics. Another consideration is, which is the most viable ethics? In any case, this theory of ethics [developed by society (as opposed to derived from nature)] would mean that ethics are a social institution developed by the society (church or government) to promote the benefit of the society. But if the ethics break down over time, as we have seen in many cases throughout history, the benefits accrue to the power elite, and or the powerful social institutions that impose the ethics (church or government), and do not end up benefiting society as a whole.

All human beings have a certain level of ethical tendency, but also desires that can cloud their intellects and allow their egoistic aspect to hold sway in their personalities. Yet, all human beings also have a deeper yearning; they desire something in higher life; that something may be seen as an overall goal or purpose in life. The purely ethical arguments have as their goal: having order, peace and prosperity for life. The religious arguments may be seen as going further. In the religious ideal the argument is that ethics or morality comes from a divine agency, and that there is a goal that rises above the temporal, finite human existence, which is to be able to live on after death, to meet God or to go to heaven, etc. So for religious morality, an unethical act is not just an act against society, but also against God, or Spirit, and so the additional concept of "sin" is added to the conceptualization. Sin may be defined as: Deliberate disobedience to the known will of God; A condition of estrangement from God resulting from such disobedience.

The previous views may be considered as the western religious conceptualization of morality and the western philosophical conceptualization of ethics. However, we may also wonder, if life is just for having order and peace as the pure ethicists might say, or to go to heaven as the religionists might say, what is the worth of being ethical if there is no order or peace, and in the case of religion, if it is so hard not to commit sins or even know if there is a real heaven? Specifically, if as the secular ethicist advocates, one will lead an ethical life only to die and have nothing in the end [after death], why should one be ethical at all? If it is too hard to be sinless as the religionist advocates, and since there is no knowledge of life after death, why worry about being moral? Why not "live it up?" Why not break laws and live unethically, if it will bring more pleasure and wealth and make life more enjoyable before the inevitable end? As to the religionist argument that life is to lead to heaven, why should a person believe that at all? Why not make up a rationalization, as most people do, that there are small sins and big ones, and small ones are okay, and will be forgiven, or excuse the sins altogether as "errors of the flesh" and hold on to the expectation of going to heaven because they are 'believers' of the faith who will go to heaven, as opposed to others who will go to hell for being unbelievers (even if they lived an ethical life), etc. Why should a person give allegiance to a church that tells them they will get some reward in a future life, which cannot be seen or be proven to exist? Why should a poor person live ethically, but in abject poverty, hoping to have prosperity after death, while secularists and religionists espouse their theories, even as they live well or even in luxury, while the rest suffer? Why should that person not do something unethical to gain wealth and live a better life, just as other supposedly ethical secular leaders or religious people, who are part of the community and who became wealthy through unethical means {even if those means were not against the law}, do?

The secularist and religionist matrixes are based on limited and conditional argument or ideology, while the *Matrix of African Proverbs* is based on the principle of universality derived from observations of nature [natural order of Creation and the patterns of human nature]. Where does this universality come from? The answer is the insight from mystical inner experience. Mysticism, the teaching of self-discovery by finding one's higher Self and it's oneness with nature and the Divine, offers secular philosophy and religion the higher benefit of coming into higher consciousness, beyond the secular social philosophies and concepts or the tenets of religious belief (faith), and the practice of religious ritual (traditions to reinforce the religious belief system). Mysticism points to an attainment beyond worldly secular goals or orthodox phenomenological religious perspectives (eschatologies). Higher consciousness allows the experiencer to see beyond the limited scope of worldly ideals and paradigms. If the societal philosophy of a culture is guided by those who have achieved the mystical insight, the ethical construct that is used by that society will be of a higher order, transcending the dry intellectualism of non-spiritual secularity and the irrational ritualism religiosity. It will be universalistic, all-encompassing and based on eternal cosmic truth as opposed to transient, ephemeral human realities that apply to some individuals or groups or societies, but not all humanity, and are therefore limited and flawed [and unsustainable].

If ethics is an effect or outgrowth of the biological processes, how do we explain the examples of right and wrong, order and balance, found in the natural world? If we take a ,non-human example such as the growth of a tree, we can see it cannot grow anywhere. There are certain parameters, certain conditions that are necessary for it to survive and grow. If the seed falls in one place it will grow, but not in another. The stars and planets follow an order and harmony based on certain universal laws. This is the ethics of the world, the order of the world, and that exists independent of the effect of the biological processes undergone by human beings. The problem is that ethics born of biology are grounded in the phenomenological [physical realm] perspective of nature, which does have its natural order. However, that natural order does not apply to the transcendental realms; for that we need mysticism. So the ethics of the world and the ethics of the transcendent should be thought of as related but separate aspects of existence. The lower, the worldly ethics are to be mastered in order to be able to discover and understand the higher, the transcendental ethics.

The religious argument for ethics, that it was given by a God, imposes ethics based on the desires of a divine agency. The motivation for presenting laws authored and delivered by a divine agency is that it might tend to provoke greater impetus for followers to adhere to them. Often the motivation to follow such regulations is the threat of suffering imposed by the agency (wrath of the god or goddess). As most non-mystical religious texts demonstrate, the wrath of gods and goddesses can be as whimsical and arbitrary or subjective and egoistic as that of human beings. This is the disqualifier of religious motivation through fear and or guilt, the flaw of irrational sentiment born of ignorance of the higher mystical insight about the universality of all life that expresses through wisdom as compassion, understanding, and forgiveness. Neither the secular basis nor the non-secular basis of ethics that are founded in fear {ignorance} are founded in truth, because neither is universal. Rather, they are subjective, conditional, and therefore, do not meet the criteria of universality, which is intrinsically just, amply self-evident, and universally applied. Ethics founded in truth [as reflected in the natural order of Creation] ultimately needs no divine agency nor social institution as a person realizes their ethical nature that is one with the source of cosmic ethics and which places them in harmony with the human, social and cosmic worlds.

If there is a "natural" order and or truth that exists independently from human existence, what does that mean about the ethics of human beings? If the validity and utility of an ethical scheme are based on the benefits to human beings or human societies alone then it is partial, as opposed to impartial; it is shortsighted, limited, egoistic and ultimately unsustainable. In order to be sustainable, the ethics must follow universal, cosmic truths and not just subjective or conditional realities as perceived by limited and egoistic human beings. In other words, if we want to discover true ethics, we must seek that ethical construct which is universal and not conditional, an ethics that applies in the human world as well as the universe. Then we will find the consistency that transcends the contradictions of flawed human constructs. We will discover that *African Proverbial Wisdom Teachings* reflect that essential universal quality of the cosmic matrix, how it is to be applied in life, and how it is to be implemented for individual human existence and for society as well.

Another perspective is offered by ancient Mystical religion. This perspective may be considered generally as the view held by some Eastern, African and Native American religions. In the mystical format, ethics or morality [which may be used interchangeably], is seen as an emanation of nature. For example, in Ancient Egyptian religion, the earliest forces known by the people were the Nile river and the sun. The river flooded annually, bringing nutrients and replenishing the soil regularly. The sun rises daily at an appointed time. The combination of those two forces allowed life to exist. Therefore, orderliness, regularity, consistency and some mysterious power, engenders life. Thus, the idea arises that if a person were to come into that same harmony of orderliness, regularity, and consistency, then it might be possible for them to come into a higher form of life, harmony with the universe. This means coming into harmony with the world (universe) and discovering the mysterious power behind all life, and in fact, all existence. Hence, in Mystical systems, the development of ethics precedes, but is tied into, the development of Mystery systems, which involve vision quests, meditation, altered states of consciousness, and out of body (astral) experiences. So in the Mystical religious philosophies, ethics arise out of the order of the universe, and morality is an expression of the regularity [law] of nature. In other words, morals are derived from understanding the preexisting order of the universe and are not arbitrarily or logically created through reflections without taking into consideration the self-evident wisdom of nature. Amorality is therefore, when a person steps out of the order of nature, and thus, also from the operations of the Divine. Immorality is consciously going against the order of nature. Thus, the goal of the Mystical religion is not just to have order in physical human existence, but to produce a harmony and communion between the microcosm (human being) and the macrocosm (nature), in other words, between the human being and the cosmos, soul and Spirit, even before death. The Mystical religious view of the universe is that it is an expression of the Divine. This may be thought of as a pantheistic concept. In African religious systems, this paradigm may outwardly appear as a henotheistic system of religious practice, but philosophically, it is pantheistic, and more so, panentheistic. Therefore, universal human and social ethics are a foundation for human order. This allows the further movement into spiritual discovery and harmony. This in turn allows higher consciousness and the goal of life to be attained during life and after death.

## Humanitarian Ethics

Firstly, it might be well justified to say that all human cultures, at some point in their history, have established what they believe to be a moral (ethical) and principled standard for establishing and maintaining order in a society, even if they apply it to their own society and selectively to others, and even if that standard is barbarous. Nevertheless, it is some form of standard. If the criteria is not just the material well-being of oneself or one's society, but are universal and based on natural practical human needs and humanitarian wisdom, they are beneficial since they promote peace and harmony collectively. If it is not universal, it cannot be ethical by this higher understanding; therefore, it cannot be beneficial. These two principles may be termed *universal* or *humanitarian ethics* versus *egoistic ethics*. When most societies claim to have ethics, what they mostly speak of is egoistic ethics, that is, a set of rules that promote their own well-being at the expense of other societies; terms like *"national interests"* are usually code for "what is in the best interest for 'our' country or 'our' family or 'our' society," etc. The *humanitarian ethics* may be categorized as that which leads to *positive ethical conscience* for the community, society and humanity, while the *egoistic ethics* may be categorized as that which leads to *negative ethical conscience*.

The primary standard or foundation of the humanitarian ethics may be regarded as the injunction against harming others, and the highest expression of that moral sanction is to refrain from killing, and instead, caring for others. Therefore, from that highest of the humanitarian ethics we may accept the concept of non-killing as a universal canon or dictum that leads or at least should lead to peace and harmony in society. Therefore, we can say that policies and concepts that promote imbalances between genders or 'races', or injustices, disharmony, or conflicts that directly or indirectly lead to social strife and killing are anti-humanitarian ethics or ethics of a purpose other than humanitarian conceptions, functions or goals.

African ethics, as espoused by *African Proverbial Wisdom Teachings,* is born of the desire for order and harmony of social groups. That desire promotes the development of ways of understanding life (wisdom) so that life has meaning beyond simple egoistic pleasure seeking and self-satisfaction. It encourages ethical traditions (procedures for establishing social balance and rebalancing {ways to restore balance and order when the harmony is disturbed}.

This concept of ethical wisdom is founded in a practical need, but also recognizes the spiritual order that transcends the physical world. So *African Proverbial Wisdom Teachings* relate to secular and non-secular affairs, and recognize not only a religious imperative [to discover the meaning and fulfillment of the purpose of life], but also a social need [order, harmony], both best established and sustained by following a cosmic model. The ethics designed to promote conditions wherein that social need may be met are seen as beneficial because it allows the members of the society to discover the meaning and purpose of life, and to fulfill the goal of life, which is worldly order, peace and advancement, along with spiritual knowledge and establishment of the individual personality in higher spiritual existence.

## Ethics For The Leadership

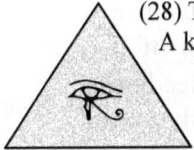

(28) The Lord of the Two Shores is one who knows,
A king who has courtiers is not ignorant...

-Instructions to Meri-Ka-Ra
[Ancient Egyptian Wisdom Texts]

Human beings need leadership. This is because they do not carry within themselves, the hereditary knowledge of their ancestors in regards to history, customs, survival skills, ethics, social skills, or religion. Every human being has a tendency towards selfish desires {vice} and a tendency towards ethics. However, each must learn, as if from scratch, the basic knowledge of the world and the wisdom of family, community and Spirit. As a civilization advances technologically, the knowledge and the capacity for dissemination changes; also older useless knowledge is no longer needed, so it is not retained. It is possible for a society to become so advanced that it forgets the pathway that led to its advancement. If something catastrophic were to

> One person alone cannot rule the country.
> - **Ethiopia proverb**

happen to such a society, its members might not know how to recover, because they forgot the history of how they developed from a primitive society to the more advanced level. Human beings are prone to forgetfulness and therefore, have a tendency to repeat errors, not having learned the wisdom of the past. This factor operates in individuals as well as societies. Leadership, at the local as well as national levels, is the key to the maintenance and transmittal of knowledge, especially relating to human identity, character (am I a member of a society, humanity or am I in it for myself) and conscience (how should all human beings be treated). If there is a lack of ethical conscience in the society, it can easily and quickly devolve to barbarism.

Human beings need positive ethical leadership to give them direction and proper examples to follow; this is true in a family as well as in a community and a society. Until a person develops with sufficient maturity to take on a role as a contributing member of society, the leadership of their family is the mother and father; the leadership of the village [community] is in the chief, elders, presidents and/or prime ministers; the leadership on the religious path is the priest or priestess. This is why when the righteous leadership of a society is disrupted, the society can fall quickly into chaos. The same can occur when the righteous leadership of a society becomes corrupt; the society can fall quickly into chaos. This explains why even societies that appear to have reached a high level of intellectual, philosophical or technological accomplishment, sometimes achieved over hundreds or even thousands of years, can descend to great depths of depravity, violence, greed, debauchery and many other degraded states of social disorder in government and economic policies that lead to atrocities, holocausts, slavery, exploitation, etc. Examples can be presented in varied parts of the world that demonstrate how societies that were previously living in accordance with ethics that,

*A people without a leader ruin the town.*
**–Ghananian proverb**

by the standard presented in this book, would be considered acceptable, if not advanced, and sustainable level of social order, descended to disorder and even chaos after being severely disrupted. For example, in several African societies, sexual restraints have fallen in societies that previously followed traditional social norms governing sexuality. The movement towards promiscuity has opened the door to the expanded rates of the spreading AIDS disease in Africa. Such social sexual disorders can also be seen in societies of the Temperate regions, in Europe and Asia, where raping can even become a tool of war, slavery and a means to commit genocide by diluting a group's ethnic appearance, together with their language and culture, so that the original people no longer exist and a new mestizo group emerges which has its allegiance to the conquering, colonial group. Likewise, after being disrupted, some societies that did not previously have a history of dictatorship or tyranny, took to those negative forms of social practices. Also, after being disrupted, some societies suddenly adopted torture and crime as accepted forms of social practice. One example of movement towards corruption and crime is Nigeria, Africa, which, by the late 20th century, had come to be known as the Credit Card Fraud capital of the world in current times, and is also the source of other rackets, frauds and drug trafficking due to the high level of corruption in business and government in the country.

So no matter how advanced a civilization may seem to be, it can always potentially fall into a primitive state if the leadership is not there in the form of wise elders, chiefs, presidents, etc., to promote the *positive ethical conscience* of the society, the traditions of social interaction, and ethical considerations that allow cooperation, civility and caring among human beings, both within societies and between societies. Though human life may not seem different from animal life, actually it can be worse. Animals do not create bombs and other weapons to kill each other because they do not have the intellectual capacity nor the egoistic awareness to see themselves as individuals with the right to see themselves as more deserving to pursue their needs and desires at the expense of the right of others to exist and pursue their own needs and desires. Accordingly, if the leadership is unrighteous, they can lead an ignorant society to errant, immoral and corrupt pursuits and eventual ruin.[104]

105

> *When emotions are societies objective, tyranny will govern regardless of the ruling class.*
> **-Ancient Egyptian proverb**

Since the leaders of a village have special power over the village by virtue of their authoritative positions, filling the roles of ethical models, directors, leaders, and in the case of Religious Council members, also wise judges and spiritual/moral guides, they set the tone, ethical boundaries, and inspire selflessness or ethical conscience, like parents, for the village, or country members or for humanity as a whole.

106

> *The heart of the wise man lies quiet like limpid water.*
> **-Cameroon proverb**

The leaders of a society, be they in the form of Council leader, king, president, prime minister, etc., should come from the ranks of those who were good followers,[107] should be humble and peaceful,[108] and should not just enjoy the benefits of leadership, but be willing to deal with the rubbish[109] of the society [negative thoughts, feelings, emotions, actions and abuses of others who act out of ignorance or lack of ethical development].

> *He whose refuses to obey cannot command.* -**Kenyan proverb**

> *A chief is like a rubbish heap; everything comes to him.*
> *A leader is a donkey for others to ride.*
> — African Proverbs

So leaders should be strong, but not necessarily in physical terms like those who are ready to fight or hurt others to demonstrate their dominance, like the top dog in a pack. Instead they should have strength of will and strength of ethical conscience.[110] The leaders should be wise and not just intellectually bright[111] but feeling with their people.[112] Leaders should also realize that those who take on the burden of responsibility for positive outcomes also will have the burden of the responsibility for the outcome if it is not successful.[113]

> *The strong do not need clubs.*
> **—Senegalese proverb**

> *A clear thinking leader is a sign of stability*
> *and an agent for change in society.*
> **—Sierra Leonean proverb**

> *To manage yourself, use your head,*
> *to manage others, use your heart.*
> **- African Proverb**

> *A person who carries responsibility also receives blame.*
> **-Kenyan proverb**

114

They require wise counsel that is based on sound African Ethics and not just in political tactic, war strategy or psychological charismatic manipulations;[115] the society guided by leaders who have not been educated in ethical wisdom can easily lead a society into conflict, violence and war especially

> Leadership does not depend on age.
> –Namibian proverb

when that society is also uneducated in such matters.[116] It is important to realize that age, in and of itself, is not a guarantee of wisdom. Barbarous societies [empires, colonial powers] may have wise elders who are wise about establishing colonialism and implementing imperialism. In societies devastated by colonialism, imperialism or other social disruptions be they through disease, war, secularism, consumerism or natural decay of societies over time [due to forgetfulness of the ethical societal philosophy] their wisdom can be interrupted and upset since the orderly process of social development, and education as well as socialization from youth to adulthood, based on their previously developed societal philosophy, was disrupted. A sign of such decay in a society is tendency to favor expediency over due deliberate process, favoring profits over human needs and favoring youth over the elderly, thus having relegated elder members of the society to marginal positions or at worse, discarding them as useless [this is the western model or the model of many, if not most, modern popular cultures].[117] The ideal leaders are knowledgeable in African proverbial wisdom and skilled in problem solving, healing the wounds of the heart and experienced in matters of parenting, and good governance.[118] That confidence inspires the general membership of the society, it demonstrates a higher way of life and provides an example of what is permissible and what is not. The ideal leaders should lead by influence, sense and goodwill and not through fear.[119] Leaders should be good listeners and not egoistic[120] or proud[121] personalities interested only in their own ideas or goals without taking into consideration the needs and concerns of others.[122] Leaders should know how to bring out the best in others without seeking constant praise or accolades for themselves and allow others to develop and become great.[123]

 [124]  [125]

This is important for the harmony and peace of the family, village or cooperative group but also for the future development of the society, as those in the next generation will one day take over the full leadership role. The leaders should not just talk about ethics and righteousness but must practice and be an example of it for their people.[126] A leader, no matter how honest or righteous or wise, cannot sustain an unrighteous society; [127] therefore it is important to promote truth, justice, ethics and education to encourage, support and maintain the development of intelligent and responsible members of society who will do their part to uphold order and support the wisdom of the wise.[128]

> *The leader who leads by pointing the way leaves no footprints for his followers.* - **African Proverb**

 [129]

There are two important components in leadership from the African Wisdom point of view: Leadership and Counselors. A good leader is someone who is not removed from the experiences of the people being led.[130] A leader does not dictate to others but works with them to develop understanding through reason and feeling.[131]

> *One head alone does not go into council.*
> *One head does not contain all the wisdom.*
> *The elders of the village are the boundaries.*
> -Ghananian proverbs

A council of elders[132] is a forum for the best ideas of society, tempered by wisdom, to be discussed and worked out for the benefit of the society as a whole; the council members are not expected to agree on every idea but to come to a consensus[133] on the best course of action[134] given the current circumstances and in keeping with the values of the society.[135] It is important to remember that in order to promote harmony and peace it is important to develop agreements that are communally discussed and deliberated.[136] This ideal of government, by the wise, has many benefits, like avoiding egoistic rulers, mobs, juntas and aristocracies that usurp the power and abuse the general population through systems such as government by military [militocracy], political parties [particracy], corporations [corpocracy], the few [oligarchy] the rich [plutocracy], tyrants [tyranny], dictators [dictatorship/despotism] or other malefactors of society.

It is important to understand that this form of government is higher than 'democracy' because democracy, as developed by western countries, and others, has been useful in providing a valuable means for skillful but unethical leaders to manipulate the majority of a country while causing them to believe that they 'democratically' chose a particular path and are in control of their own fate when in reality they are subservient to the designs of those who are in power [the rich and powerful][137]. Additionally, the idea at the center of the modern concept of 'democracy' of a majority making decisions for a whole society necessarily means that the needs and concerns of minorities will be neglected or that their rights will be ignored or violated. For this reason democracy was referred to as a *tyranny of the majority*. Nowhere in the world do we see direct democracies, where the population elects government officials and controls the agenda of the government directly; this would be 'pure' democracy. But a direct democratic system would mean that ordinary people have the power in government and not the elected officials, as in a representative system like what is used in most western countries. So it is remarkable that such a system of government was rejected by western countries in favor of republics or parliamentary systems so as to deflect the desires of majorities that might turn on them [the politicians]. Yet, the western politicians tout the benefits of 'democracy' and how all countries should have 'democratic' systems of government. Nevertheless, the very same system that protects aristocracies and plutocracies ['democracy'] also allows factions of those groups to wrest control and impose their will, the will of the power elite of the society, on the rest which is actually the majority in terms of number. Thus, such 'democracies' as that used in the U.S.A., often referred to as a 'representative democracy' or a 'republic', are actually tyrannies of the majority but not in the way meant by political philosophers such as Alexis de Tocqueville or John Stuart Mill.

The ideal form of government advocated by African wisdom may be termed *Wisdocracy*. This form of government as expressed in African Wisdom would be linked to a system whereby positions are assigned by merit [meritocracy] as opposed to nepotism or some other unethical and or immoral criteria. Instead of a government system [democracy] that supposedly establishes general will [over 50% of a population] over individual rights and minority rights, and seeing that as 'the common' [collective] good, the African system of government advocated in the *Proverbial Wisdom Teachings* promotes the good of the collective over the individual right of deviation from the collective good, which at the same time promotes the good for the individual as well as society as a collective. Here, in the African conception of government by council of elders [the wise] the good of the collective and that of the individual are the same while the freedom promoted in western styled democracies promoted individual freedoms at the expense of society and the general will of a majority over the freedoms of the individual or minority groups. This fatal flaw of democracy has been described as *tyranny of the majority*.

The phrase **"tyranny of the majority,"** was used in criticizing democracy and majority rule where decisions made by a majority within that system would constitute the placement of the interests of that majority above a minority's interest so much that it could be comparable to the operations of tyrannical despots.[138]

The concept was alluded to by Plato in his book, Republic. The phrase was used by Alexis de Tocqueville in his work, *Democracy in America* (1835, 1840). It was also popularized by John Stuart Mill, in his book *On Liberty* (1859), citing de Tocqueville. The *Federalist Papers[139]* in the United States of America frequently cite the concept, but usually referring to it by the name of "the violence of majority faction".

Jean-Jacques Rousseau's doctrine of the 'general will' ends in a tyranny of the majority. Supposedly, by subordinating their rights to the 'general will,' the individuals are thereby 'forced to be free'. The political philosophy concept of a **general will** (*volonté générale*), in the context of Rousseau's argument, refers to the desire, will or interest of a people as a whole, or, as referred to in the U.S. constitution as, the "general welfare". In this concept by Rousseau, the "general will" is equated as being identical to the rule of law[140], and to the *mens una* of Spinoza.[141]

> The notion of the general will is wholly central to
> Rousseau's theory of political legitimacy . . . . from the
> *Discourse on Political Economy*, where Rousseau

emphasizes that the general will exists to protect individuals against the mass, not to require them to be sacrificed to it. He is, of course, sharply aware that men have selfish and sectional interests which will lead them to try to oppress others. It is for this reason that loyalty to the good of all alike must be a supreme (although not exclusive) commitment by everyone, not only if a truly general will is to be heeded but also if it is to be formulated successfully in the first place".[142]

Firstly, Rousseau's concept of *general will* cannot be defined as the 'desire, will or interest of a people as a whole' because in a large society [especially multicultural, multiethnic] there can be no singular direction or understanding of issues. There would always be dissent so there can be no ideal of a 'whole' in a political process that proceeds from a 'democratic' vote since there would be no need for a vote if there was a singular whole desire or will of the people. Therefore, if the desire or will of a group is made into law that disparity becomes enforced institutionally. Thus, such a society becomes an institutional tyranny where the majority group [those who won the vote with over 50% of the votes] governs through a tyrannical system of government [forcing their will on those who only gained 49% or less of the vote] as opposed to an individual tyrant who would govern likewise but as an individual. Rousseau's ideal of 'loyalty to the good of all alike' is also flawed because it leaves the application of the welfare of the whole to the ethics of the majority who are composed of all kinds of people ranging from egoistically ethical to the ethically conscientious. So the 'commitment by everyone' [either in the group of those who won or those who lost] is impossible since there will always be [in any group based on political agendas and partisan interests] those who care only about their own desires and also, those who have been tyrannized (those in the minority who had the desires of the majority imposed on them) would have been excluded, developing resentments, grudges and the desire to be equally tyrannical and or corrupt when they get their chance. Finally, in the statement, 'not only if a truly general will is to be heeded but also if it is to be formulated successfully in the first place' the idea presupposes that a viable general will was devised from the beginning but how is that possible if the rights of minorities are excluded from the beginning? Is the group as a whole supposed to agree in the beginning that this is a good system and that when disparities occur the minorities are to accept their fate and bee good losers [until they get their chance to win whenever]?

The concept of the *tyranny of the majority*, as used by the political philosophers named above refers to a majority of the population [over 50%] imposing their will on the minority [group of people numbering less than 50%]. Actually, in the western styled 'democracies' the masses of people included in the numerical majority, who supposedly won the vote and who supposedly would impose their will on the minority] do not control the policies of the government since it is the representatives, they vote for, who make the decisions [regardless of the intent expressed in the supposedly democratic vote]. So, the concept of the *tyranny of the majority* is actually incorrect. Thus, such 'democracies' as that used in the U.S.A., often referred to as a 'representative democracy' or a 'republic', are actually **tyrannies of the minority** since the desires or will of the minority of people who are in power, those who control the finances and who becomes a political candidate and who is funded to run a political campaign and be 'elected', impose their will on the majority through their control of the economy and the politicians.

The point is that democracies are not viable systems of government, though they may be expedient in allowing policies to be pursued. A system of government composed of a council and government by consensus was used in Africa with many variations. The example of the traditional government that was used in Botswana was presented in an earlier volume.[143] The consensus building process is the best way to promote harmony and the prevention of

108

tyranny in a society by any group. Consensus building prevents the development of factions, partisanship or other forms of segmentation in a society because it precludes conditions that would lead to people feeling alienated, abused [*tyrannized*]. The dictionary presents the antonym of *tyranny* as *democracy;* however, as we have seen, democracy is a kind of modified tyranny. The better antonym for *tyranny* is *consensus*. *Consencracy* or government by consensus does not include political parties or formal oppositions. Consensus models of discourse in consensus government require that a true consensus be reached by those in a society who are discussing the political agenda of their society, though the implementation of the policies advanced by consensus may be decided upon by majority vote in the legislature, which is encouraged and expected to pass only regulations that are generally truly approved by those who have engaged in the consensus building political discussions throughout the country.[144]

 145  146

The ideal is a situation in which leaders are held to a higher standard and the willful breach of the ethical standard shall because enough for removal from a leadership position for a period of time and may include lifetime banishment. In African culture based on *Proverbial Wisdom*, the leaders, being not only secular philosophers but also spiritual guides have a greater responsibility to maintain an ethical standard. Since they occupy the highest offices in the society, those who have committed a serious enough breach of ethics cannot be allowed to occupy any Council position. This removal will protect the integrity of the Council, which is so important to the ethical framework of the entire society.

147

If these tenets of leadership were followed, then such leaders could claim greatness in leadership. And, the society they are leading would develop towards true civilization and away from barbarism.

> *If two wise men always agree, then there is no need for one of them.*
> —Zambian proverb

## ROYALTY IN AFRICAN CULTURE AND AFRICAN PHILOSOPHY

In ordinary popular culture the usual idea about royalty is that they are a special 'kind' of people as in a class on to themselves or even a special 'breed' of human, better than the rest, and or that have been perhaps divinely appointed and should be accorded special and perhaps even absolute authority in all matters.[148] This special deference is accorded regardless of their worthiness, education or character simply because of their ancestry. This ideal held true in the concept of the royalty of many European nations, and Asiatic nations including the Roman Empire.

When we see rituals or public ceremonies in African nations in modern times the people who are considered royalty seem to be accorded that same kind of deference. They may be seen clad in special clothing and adorning themselves with gold and jewels. Individuals may be seen prostrating before them, swearing allegiance or otherwise paying their respects.

*African Proverbial Wisdom Teachings* present a different perspective on royalty. Firstly, royal personalities do not have absolute power. They are to be accorded respect because of the position itself but in order to keep their position they must uphold certain ethical standards. Otherwise they may be removed and that removal may be by force if necessary. So the idea of hereditary lineage to the throne or its adjunct concept of **Primogeniture** [the common law right of the firstborn son to inherit the entire estate, to the exclusion of younger siblings] does not apply in the higher application of African Proverbial Wisdom. However, it is also important to realize that just because a person may sit in a royal throne that does not mean that they should necessarily be respected.[149] It takes more than

111

just sitting on a throne to be a royal, this includes good character, training and good counselling.

The most powerful African kings and queens, the Pharaohs of Ancient Egypt, were not absolute monarchs but answered to a council of priests and priestesses who were themselves trained in spiritual ethical philosophy [Maat philosophy].[150]

*A large chair does not make a king.* – Sudanese proverb

So, a king or queen should have competent advisors.[151] But this ideal of advisors, should not be equated with that of modern times where the royalty, or presidents, prime ministers, etc. can listen to advice, ignore the will of the people, as expressed through elections or other means of expression, and then do whatever they want to do after that; their decisions must be bound by the ethical wisdom. The councillors present an accord[152] on an issue and clarify how a decision is impacted by the ethical wisdom teaching and through reasoned reflection based on the ethical wisdom a proper decision will be arrived at.

Kings and queens are human beings like everyone else;[153]/[154]/[155]/[156]/[157] therefore they have the same capacities and weaknesses and thus should not be treated as special human beings above others. Also, in African Proverbial Wisdom, non-royalty members of the society are not encouraged to cultivate irrational adulation of royalty and African Proverbial Wisdom does not support the modern practice of celebrity worship as is practiced in modern culture.[158] The king and the people should share a common fate.[159] Unlike societies where the rich and powerful can insulate themselves from the troubles and economic downturns that affect the general population [as is common in many countries that practice capitalism and or market economics, caste systems and or racism]; otherwise the royalty will act independently, eventually becoming corrupt and

*A canoe does not know who is king - when it turns over, everyone gets wet.* – Wolof proverb implementing policies that are to their benefit at the expense of the rest. All members of society, including those who are in leadership positions, should not be insulated from the fate of the whole population; in this way the interests of leaders and those in power will coincide with the interests and needs of the whole population.

*Even the king needs to be taught. - Somali proverb*

Those who are selected to be royalty cannot be of low character.[160] Royalty, like everyone else, need to be properly reared and cultured in the traditions and wisdom of the society and trained in the practice of politics and sustainable social management.[161] Therefore, they need to be advised and guided about issues in order to carry out their duties in a manner that will sustain the needs[162] of the people and allow the continued sustenance of the population and existence of the king and queen in their positions.[163/164]

So, in traditional African culture, the royalty owe their position to the people and must act in accordance with the parameters set out by the councillors which are in keeping with the values of the society [societal philosophy].[165]

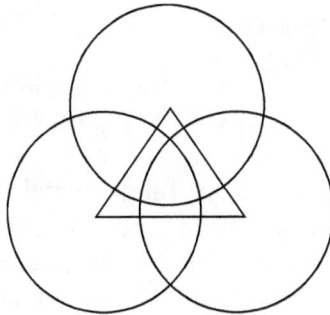

# CHAPTER 3: RESPONSIBILITIES TO FAMILY, COMMUNITY AND SELF.

(5) The wise one is a [teacher] to the nobles.
Those who know that he knows will not attack him,
No [crime or injustice] occurs when a wise one is near; justice comes to them distilled,
In the form of the sayings of the ancestors.
Copy your fathers, your ancestors,

(6) See that the their wise words endure in books,
Open them and read them, copy their knowledge,
they who are taught become skilled.
Don't act with evil, kindness is an expression of good nature,
Make your memory last through love of you.
Increase the [people], befriend the town,
God will be praised for (your) donations,
One will ------
Praise your goodness,
Pray for your health

-Instructions to Meri-Ka-Ra
[Ancient Egyptian Wisdom Texts]

Since there are three fundamental relationships in African Culture there are ethical responsibilities related to each one for the purpose of fomenting the proper development and fulfillment of each relationship. Before outlining the responsibilities of each area of human relations we will first undergird that framework with a foundation in *African Ethical Conscience* which will manifest ideally as ethical conscientiousness when a human being engages in socially required relations.

# Childhood, Adulthood and Eldership in African Socio-Ethical tradition.

In African social tradition, the burden of responsibility falls on all members of society but adults have the added responsibility to care for the children[166] and for the elders. When a human being is born he or she is to be cared for by the adults. When he or she grows up they are to take care of their children and their parents, the adults who took care of them and who have now become elders. When they become elders they are to be taken care of by their children who have now become adults, and so on.[167]

**Table 4: Blueprint Component of African Society based on The Generational Responsibilities**

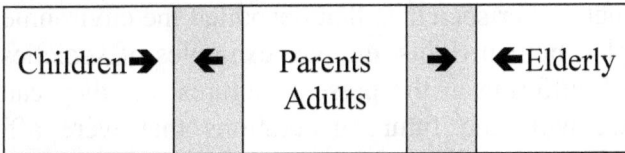

| Children➔ | ← | Parents Adults | ➔ | ←Elderly |
|---|---|---|---|---|

Ethical relations between individual members of a society, members in a community or in a society as well as relations between an individual and the Spirit are predicated upon respect; among other things, respect manifests as minding one's own business[168] and not gossiping or being a busybody, into other people's affairs[169] and also it requires forgiveness of other people's errors and trespasses. The quality and longevity of a society depends on its capacity to care for those in need. A society who's people care only for their own well-being, at the expense or exclusion of that of others, eventually degenerates into a selfish culture where the needs of its own citizens are unmet and the needs of others outside the society receive even less attention. There are many people who, after a time, become disappointed by and disillusioned with politics; they know society is destructive and unjust, they do not have faith in politicians but yet still strive to maintain the society so that they and their family may continue to live at least at their current standard of living, even at the expense of others. This way of being focuses on the personal practical well-being and sets aside the ethical/moral issues related to the reality of the destruction of the environment, the trampling of other peoples rights and the suffering that will come to future generations just so that those who understand that their culture is on an immoral/unethical path, but who do not act to stop it but rather support and perpetuate it, may not need to be inconvenienced by social disruptions. Here the caring for self and the personal family is stronger than the caring for the extended family of humanity; in this way many destructive societies have caused harm to their own citizens and the populations of other cultures; some have even self-destructed because of this negative way of living. Those societies that became empires or which otherwise came to dominate other societies, that despoiled the environment or trampled human rights, etc. are examples of societies that caused suffering in the present cultures that they came in contact with and future generations that were affected thereafter.

It is important to understand that the advancement of ethics is incomplete without it's full application; the willful support of prosperity for some at the expense of others is always incompatible with evolved ethical conscience; it is only a partial attainment that fails to lead an individual to the full development of a virtuous personality and will also fail to advance civility, compassion and harmony for society and a healthy environment for all to live in. It is also important to develop social institutions and infrastructures that allow all to live in peace by having sufficient food, being free from the elements and the injustices of life[170] so that each member of society alive now, and those who may come in the future, may have an opportunity to experience peace and harmony as well as freedom from the lack of basic necessities for life and freedom from exploitation, in order to be able to fulfill their purpose in life.

> *The house-roof fights with the rain, but he who is sheltered ignores it.*
> —Wolof proverb

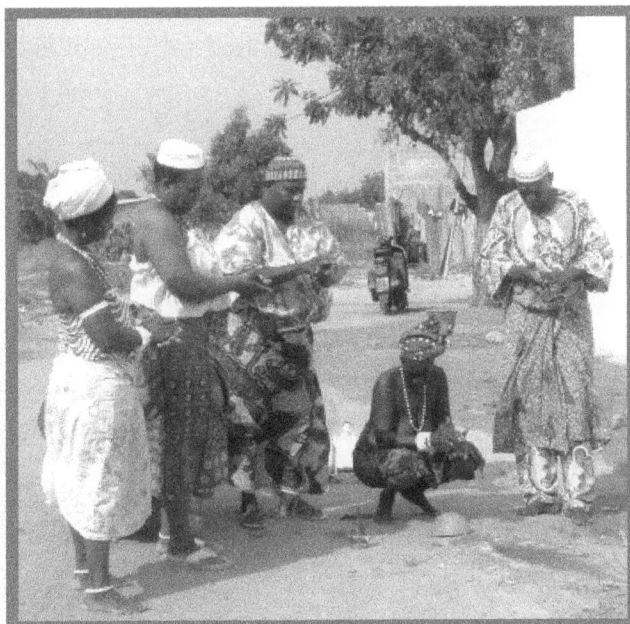

**Figure 19:** African Traditional Priests and Priestesses

**Table 5: Blueprint Component of African Society based on Human Relations, Responsibilities and Regulations**

| Relations➜ | ➜ | Responsibilities | ➜ | Regulations |
|---|---|---|---|---|
| Family | ➜ | Family | ➜ | Family |
| Community | ➜ | Community | ➜ | Community |
| Spirit | ➜ | Spirit | ➜ | Spirit |

What follows is an outline for the framework of African society based on *African Proverbial Wisdom* wherein the

117

three relationships in human existence are recognized. These lead to the assignment of responsibilities each human being has for the purpose of fulfilling the relationship in question. Each responsibility is governed by a regulation {or set of regulations} that are not designed to be punitive (to punish after an infraction) but rather as guiding principles designed to be preventative, restorative and sustaining so as to help a human being take the proper course of action to achieve the desired fulfillment and or to correct from a straying path.

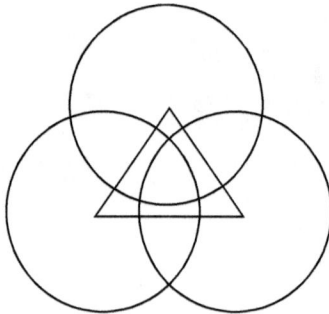

# Responsibilities related to the Relationship of Family

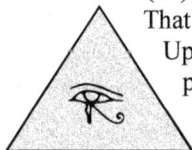

(11) Speak truth in your house,
That the officials of the land may respect you;
Uprightness befits the lord, The front of the house
puts fear in the back.

-Instructions to Meri-Ka-Ra
[Ancient Egyptian Wisdom Texts]

This section presents an outline of essential responsibilities of family for anyone who wants to create or sustain a society based on *African Proverbial Wisdom Teachings*.

171

## 1. Responsibilities related to the Concept of family - The human in relation to the human world[172]

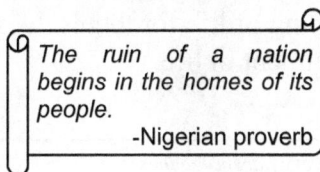

> The ruin of a nation begins in the homes of its people.
> -Nigerian proverb

1.1. In reference to the family, a human being has the responsibility to care and provide for the health and development needs of their family.

1.1.1. The main duty of children is to respect, follow the advice,[173] serve[174] and obey[175] their elders.[176]

> *It is the duty of children to wait on elders, and not the elders on children.*
> -Ashanti Ghana proverb

1.1.2.  Children are a priority in the African family and they require tender care.[177] The most responsibility rests with adults who are expected to take care of the children[178] of their immediate family and if necessary the needs of minors in their extended family (the community).[179]

> *Love is like a baby: it needs to be treated tenderly.*  -
> Ethiopia proverb

> *He who learns, teaches.*
> -Ethiopia proverb

1.1.3.  The adults are responsible for teaching their children what they need to know to survive[180] and also what they need to know in order to understand the purpose of life and pursue the meaning of life for themselves and discover fulfillment in life.[181]

> *Every parent teaches as they act.  They will speak to the children so that they will speak to their children. They will set an example and not give offence.*
> –Ancient Egyptian Proverb.

1.1.4.  Contrary to Western or other modern popular culture formats, the format of the responsibility over raising children does not fall exclusively on the individual parents but rather all parents are responsible to provide a proper environment [village] for all children.[182]

> *It takes a village to raise a child.*
> -West African proverb
> (Yoruba)

> A child who doesn't listen to its mother will be brought up by the street.
> —Sierra Leon Proverb

1.1.5.  The adults are also responsible for respecting[183] their elders and seeing to the needs of their parents, the elders and considering their advice carefully when deliberating on issues in life. Adults should not be arrogant⚭[184], thinking they know enough to make any decision on their own and that they do not need suggestions from their parents or elders. A mature adult should know that there is a difference between knowledge and wisdom and therefore value the counsel of their elders.[185]

[186]

> *Kneeling you eat with others, keep standing and you eat nothing.*
> —Tonga proverb

> *The bird that knows is different from the bird that understands.*
> -Sierra Leon proverb

1.1.5.1.  Structure of African Family responsibility. So, adults are responsible for taking care of the young and the elderly. When the Adults become elderly it is the responsibility of the young who are now adults to assume their new role and so on.

1.1.6.  Parents are to be respected even if they lose their youth and vitality.[187] The main responsibility of the elders, once they have fulfilled their duty of raising their children to adulthood, is to provide an example of a successful ethical life as an ideal for the family and society and assist the adults by guiding them with wisdom.[188] So the elders are revered for their wisdom.[189] They should not be patronized.[190]

> *Even though your mother has gray hair, she is still your mother.*
> —Tonga proverb

> *The death of an elderly man is like a burning library*
> -Ivorian proverb

1.1.6.1.    Special high regard is reserved for those members of society who have achieved high ethical standard and service to humanity.[191] They are to be seen as the guardians of life and the knowledge of what is beyond the village and to be sought out in relation to the wisdom and traditions but also how to handle the world.[192]

> *A man who pays respect to the great paves the way for his own greatness.*
> -African Proverb

> *The elders of the village are the boundaries.*
> —Ghananian proverb

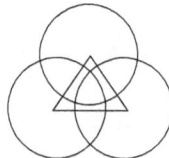

193    194    195

# Responsibilities related to the Relationship of village

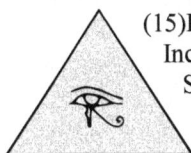

(15)Raise your youths and the residence will love you,
   Increase your subjects with friendship,
     See, your city is full of new growth.
                -Instructions to Meri-Ka-Ra
                [Ancient Egyptian Wisdom Texts]

This section presents an outline of essential responsibilities of village {community} for anyone who wants to create or sustain a society based on *African Proverbial Wisdom Teachings*.

## 2. Responsibilities related to the Concept of village - The human in relation to the social world.

> *When the village chief himself goes around inviting people to a meeting, know there is something wrong with the system.*
> –Malawian proverb

2.1. A society needs trained people to fill key roles.[196] Human beings are born in the world and cannot survive without relationships; with righteous relationships a human being can develop to the full capacity. Without those relationships the individual is limited.[197] Also, it is important to understand that every individual has value and should not be left out of the active participation in the sustenance and benefits of the community.[198]

> *Want to go fast travel alone, want to go far travel with others* -African Proverb

> *Even a good-for-nothing fellow can carry a pot of palm wine to the funeral.*
> - Ewe proverb

2.2. A village is composed of the leadership [chief, elders, teachers,[199] parents, etc.] and the group.[200] The well-being of the village is dependent upon the quality of the foundation of the village in ethics and fairness based on the ethical societal philosophy and supported by the *positive ethical conscience* of the leaders.[201]

> *A village without a leader is destroyed by a single enemy* -African Proverb

> *When your neighbor is wrong you point a finger, but when you are wrong you hide.* -Ekonda proverb

2.3. The foundation of a community in harmony and prosperity is working towards justice and humility.[202]

> *Equality is difficult but superiority is painful* -African Proverb

2.4. A human being may bring certain tendencies into the world with them when they are born and then the socialization process molds them into members of a particular society with particular values. The effects of these two factors on the development, character and behavior of a human being is sometimes referred to as the "nature vs. nurture" question. Since culture is not hereditary and must be learned, then it follows that a society's advancements are not automatically passed on from one generation to the next. This therefore means that the leaders of society are responsible for maintaining and preserving and passing on the cultural knowledge to the young. This duty is an ethic of culture. Culture is everything a people do that allows them to relate to the world, survive and understand their place within the family of humanity. The culture of a people involves language, myth, technology, religion, government and even every day things like the kind of cookware, style of cooking, clothing, transportation, traditions, entertainments, etc. that a people create and use.

> *What you expect others to do for you, do for them also*
> – Tonga proverb

2.5. In reference to the community, a human being has the responsibility to care and provide for the needs of the community and not just for their own desires or the desires or well being of their own family. This is the duty of service to humanity.[203]

> Never befoul the water. Do not lay waste the ploughed lands.
> -Ancient Egyptian Proverbs

2.6. In a wider context this means protecting the community resources, promoting sustainable enterprises and other activities that will allow the community to prosper and not run out of resources for its survival.[204]

> *The family is like a forest, if you are outside it is dense, if you are inside you see that each tree has its own position.*
> -Akhan proverb

2.7. This also means promoting the conditions that will allow members of the community to find their place[205] in the community and that their value to the community may be expressed so that they may be able to pursue their personal goals of harmonious relations with family, community and spirit. This is an ideal of progress wherein God has given the raw materials and men and women are to use those to create order and provide for the necessities of life, through proper care and distribution of those resources.[206]

> God made the sea, we make the ship;
> He made the wind, we make the sail;
> He made the calm, we make the oars.
> – Swahili proverb

2.8. Members of the society also have the responsibility to be informed and select and/or elect qualified [ethical, wise, etc.] leaders to lead them[207] and which they can rely on.[208]

> Bad leaders are elected by poor citizens who do not vote.
> -Kenyan proverb

2.9. Those in charge of resolving disputes should take care to allow everyone a good hearing; this alone may resolve many issues.[209]

> When the heart overflows, it comes out through the mouth.
> -Ethiopian proverb

# Conflict and Friction in Society

> *Two buttocks cannot*
> *avoid friction.*
> -Tonga proverb

African Proverbial Wisdom is not a panacea. It does not hold that people are all saints or that all can be completely ethical at the same time since all are on an individual as well as collective journey and all are evolving at different paces. Therefore, conflict, friction, and animosities are to be expected, from time to time, given the makeup of ordinary human nature. Within this context, misunderstandings between human beings are unavoidable.[210]

> *Trees that are together*
> *brush against each other.*
> -Tonga proverb

However, it is evident that when a society is guided by wise principles and principled people the conflicts of that society can be resolved and harmony can be restored. So, people who live together may develop conflicts due to personality issues or disagreements over other causes. However, they are to be guided so that they may discover the means to resolve their issues. The primary foundation of conflict resolution is the promotion of positive ethical culture, truth, justice, self-knowledge and fulfillment of the three relationships. This is the primary goal of *African Proverbial Wisdom Teachings*. For resolving difficulties, the wise counsel should be sought[211] and heeded;[212] otherwise those who do not seek it will lead themselves to trouble in life.[213] How does this ideal translate into governance of a society?

214

215

According to *African Proverbial Wisdom Teachings* there should be solidarity and cooperation in the community. Once all sides are heard and their concerns taken into account the Council of Elders makes a determination of what is best for all. This way, the wise elders make the decision as opposed to ignorant masses who might listen to charismatic but ill intended leaders, or they may act out of fear, prejudices or other human failings. The wise can bring together peoples hearts by remaining above purely political or egoistic motivations that may be partisan, unjust or immature. In this way, though it might not appear thus, the needs of individuals are also met. In societies that stress the fulfillment of individual needs through personal freedoms the tendency is to unbind individual pursuits of self-satisfaction which more often than not lead to antisocial behaviors and harm to other individuals or the environment due to lack of societal controls. In the context of *African Proverbial Wisdom Teachings* the needs of all are cared for, thus allowing what is individually necessary and proper to be manifested in such a way that harmony is maintained with the whole.

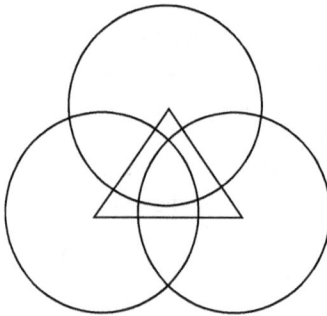

 216  217  218  219

 220  221  222  223

# Responsibilities related to the Relationship to Spirit

This section presents an outline of essential responsibilities of Spirit for anyone who wants to create or sustain a society based on *African Proverbial Wisdom Teachings*.

3. <u>Responsibilities related to the Concept of connection to the universal divine that expresses as all nature and transcendental of nature - The human in relation to the spiritual world.</u>

3.1. There is an innate desire in a person of wise development to discover the transcendental aspects of existence, to go beyond ordinary human existence in order to satisfy the spiritual need of life, which cannot be fulfilled by worldly actions or attainments,[224] and which also cannot be effectively pursued if the basic relations of life are not satisfied. Once the ordinary needs of life are satisfied and the practical realities of life are well ordered, the wise more intensively seek the answers to the important questions of life like, who am I beyond my identity as a member of this family, this community, this culture, this humanity? How did I come to exist? What is existence? Who is God and Where may I find Her?

As I get older and closer to death how may I secure my place with the Divine? Etc.

> *The wise aim at boundaries beyond the present; they transcend the parameters of their origins.*
> —African Proverb

3.2. African religion recognizes that God is everywhere and thus involved with all affairs of nature and human existence.[225]

> *If you want to send a message to God, tell it to the wind*
> -Ga proverb

3.3. African spirituality recognizes that God is imperceptible to the gross senses but can be discovered by inner development and sensitivity.[226]

> *God conceals himself from the mind of man, but reveals himself to his heart.*
> —African Proverb

3.4. As stated earlier, in reference to the spirit, a human being has the responsibility to promote spiritual development in life. This is the need for discovering the fundamental questions of life, "Who am I?", Why am I here?", "What is my purpose?", etc.[227] Ethical life and study of the Proverbial Wisdom Teachings are ways in which a person prepares for the higher spiritual discoveries of life but also experiencing the frustrations and sorrows of life is a necessary aspect of human maturity and spiritual education. Suffering in life is a way in which the world causes human beings to turn to ethical, moral and spiritual matters and not become arrogant[228] and egoistic.[229]

> *To deny God's existence is like jumping with your eyes closed.* –Malagasy proverb

> *Horns which are put on do not stick properly.*
> - South African proverb

3.5. The answers to these questions is a journey that begins with the teachings contained in myth, ritual in religion, and practiced in cultural traditions of day to day life and explained by the elders. It is nurtured by a life of ethical conduct that purifies the heart and mind and opens up deeper realms of inner feeling and psycho-spiritual insight.

> "Consume pure foods and pure thoughts with pure hands, adore celestial beings, become associated with wise ones: sages, saints and prophets; make offerings to GOD."
> - Ancient Egyptian proverb

3.6. This responsibility involves learning about spirit, making rituals to appease {make peace with/heal the rift between the individual and the universal} spirit and finally to discover and experience spirit. This is the purpose of African Religions and in this context we may refer to African Religion in the singular, reflecting the commonality of concept and purpose throughout African Religions.

Now that we have introduced the triune human relations and the ideals of responsibility, how do these fit together? Below is a diagram of that architecture based on what we have learned so far.

**Figure 20: The Architecture of African Proverbial Wisdom Teachings: Combining the Blueprints Part 1- Human Relations and Their Expansive Qualities**

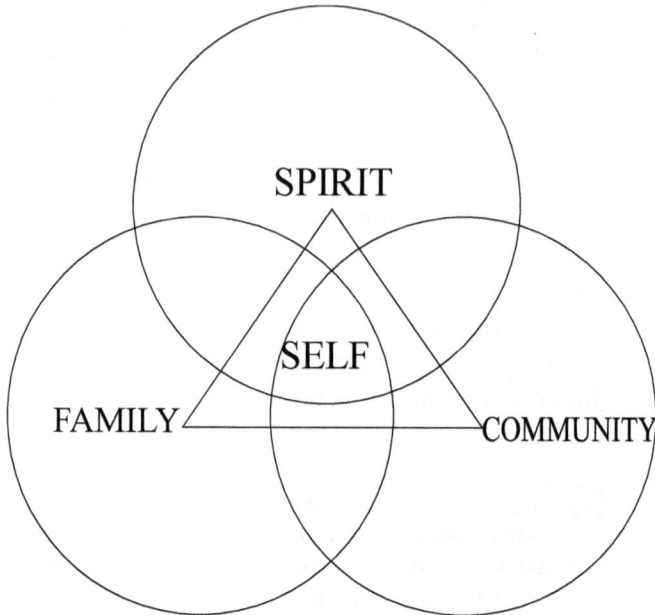

The human being is an entity composed of Self as an individual but also connected with the Creation through relationships with family, community and spirit. Those connections expand the personality so that it may encompass Creation which is it's innate but as yet undiscovered reality. The purpose of the Proverbial Wisdom is twofold, to promote harmony in the relationships so that that harmony may give way to the realization of Self not only as relator but as related, as not just the self but also the family members, the community members and with the spirit, including that which is beyond the physical reality and which lives on after the physical death of the body.

# CHAPTER 4:
# REGULATIONS BASED ON THE TRIUNE CONCEPTUALIZATIONS OF AFRICAN ETHICAL PHILOSOPHY

*A person who delays correcting things will end up crying.*
-Tonga proverb

230

**A**n organization seeking to base their ethical standards on the Triune Conceptualizations of African Ethical Philosophy may follow the model set forth in *African Proverbial Wisdom Teachings*. The concept of the three relationships in African life charges a human being who is member of the society with three areas of responsibility that are to be upheld. For each area of responsibility there are regulations and there are consequences for the inability to uphold the regulation.

The regulations below are primary ethical applications of the Responsibilities based on the Triune Conceptualizations of African Ethical Philosophy. Thus, specific situations occurring in modern society will be covered by one of the core essential principles exhorted by each conceptualization. Since African society is inclusive there

133

is a strong effort to retain members of the community by establishing methods to reconcile those who have strayed from the responsibilities of life; the deviation by a member of the community from upholding their duties is first confronted with admonition, then penalty and finally expulsion from the family, or community. In some cases incarceration may be considered. The expulsion may be considered as a high penalty. One of the worst punishments for violation of the ethical code of a society would be expulsion from the society one has grown up in and which is all one knows.

 231   232

Capital punishment may not be considered by an ideal African society since the use of capital punishment in most modern societies is predicated upon the pathological nature of society itself, which produces highly deviant mental states[233] as well as the pathological desire, on the part of ordinary members of society, to see revenge instead of rehabilitation and reconciliation. It is important to note that oftentimes society has some complicity in the deviation of it's members, perhaps by allowing unrighteous elements to persist in the society or by promoting unethical goals and values of life, for the general population to believe in and follow. These unethical goals and values of life may be present due to the barbarous nature of the society and its consequent socially degraded condition. Thus, deficient societies have some responsibility for the development of highly deviant crimes, hardened criminals and high recidivism due to the inability or unwillingness to provide proper conditions for the development of ethical and well integrated members of society and when necessary redress the errors of society that contributed to the development of those individuals

*Do not kill, it does not serve you. Punish with beatings, with detention, Thus will the land be well ordered...*
—Ancient Egyptian Proverb

who broke the ethical code of the society and then to heal and reintegrate the violators back into society. The inability or unwillingness to rehabilitate and reintegrate members of the society and the production of deviant individuals in the first place is evidence of a diseased society with deficient ethics and social values.

> *Do not kill, it does not serve you.*
> *Punish with beatings, with detention,*
> *Thus will the land be well ordered...*
> —Ancient Egyptian Proverb

Proper behavior in all relationships of life is the key to success in life and in spiritual evolution. Primarily, *African Proverbial Wisdom Teachings* exhort to everyone the need to exercise proper behavior in order to promote harmony and less "trouble" in life; this means that one should not act with impulsiveness[234] but rather, one should act with caution and then one will live longer.

> *A cautious deer grows*
> *longer horns.*
> —Tonga proverb

Those in a society who are responsible for administering the ethical code should take care to realize that in order to be effective and accepted by all, the regulations [laws] of a society must apply to all members of society be they rich or poor, male or female, etc.[235]

> *The law is a spider's web;*
> *only the little insects get*
> *caught in it.*
> -Gambian proverb

135

Regulations can be implemented in a progressive manner depending on the severity of the breakdown in responsibility. The regulations are to be administered by the council of elders and implemented by their appointed officers. The administration is firstly preventative; by making sure that the society has the three basic elements of human sustenance [food, shelter, opportunity] this in itself will act as a preventative. This means that a society should be weary and vigilant about the governance of it's people; the degree of fairness of the laws as well as the principles and traditions upon which they are based should be constantly monitored to detect any cultural degeneration or the need to change laws to meet the needs of the current generation. This vigilance is important because what is promoted by the societal philosophy of a culture becomes endemic in the cultural value system of a society and if it is a negative tendency it can become entrenched and difficult to change. The forces that cause cultural values to be deep-rooted and well-established can include vested interests of individuals or groups in a society who have something to gain by keeping the 'status quo' or self-centeredness of the individuals of a society who support certain policies as a group, perhaps due to ignorance, pleasure seeking, the hope to become one of the privileged class, etc. It is important to keep in mind that *African Proverbial Wisdom* is not compatible with the notion of social classes in a manner that produces aristocracies, nobilities, serfs, underprivileged or permanent under-classes, etc.

236

Another preventative is the education of all members of society in the *societal philosophy* that is based on objective ethical wisdom. As stated earlier, a *Societal Philosophy* that recognizes the spiritual connection between all life and the existence of spiritual dimensions beyond the physical world will lead to a culture that develops institutions to promote ethics, justice and the protection of nature. This is a civilized culture. Concomitantly, the society should be versed in the *societal myth,* which informs the people of their social origins, language, legacy, spiritual heritage and collective purpose in life. These bring meaning and stability to life, lessening the need for stealing and the development of pathological personalities that are prone to crime, violence and or drug abuse.

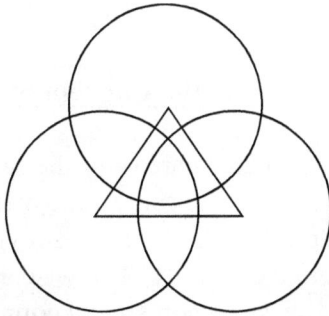

# Regulations in the area of family

This section presents an outline of essential regulations {laws, rules, guidelines} of family based on the responsibilities to family for anyone who wants to create or sustain a society based on *African Proverbial Wisdom Teachings*.

1. <u>**Regulations based on the Concept of family**</u>

1.1. The failure to take care of or the failure to make an honest effort to take care of the members of one's family should be considered as a violation of the African ethic of family. The wise are ready to forgive,[237] first admonish and counsel; then warn and finally take strong action. Adult members of the family are charged with the responsibility of providing for the needs of the children and elders, to protect, clothe, feed and educate them. The elders assist them. However, the general conditions of the community do have an effect on the family. If a society is constituted in such a format that prevents people from acquiring the necessary opportunities for advancing themselves and or providing for their basic needs then that society is not operating in accordance with the African ethic of village (Community) and should be corrected.

> *He who forgives ends the argument*
> -African Proverb

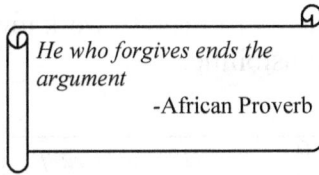

1.1.1. The violator should be issued an admonishment with counseling and recommended action that he or she can take to redress the violation along with a recommendation of how the society can assist the violator to understand the problem and correct it.

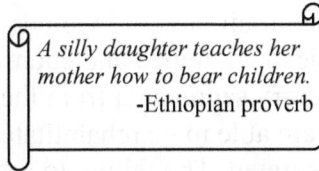

> *A silly daughter teaches her mother how to bear children.*
> -Ethiopian proverb

1.2. Children should not be arrogant.[238] Children should be protected and not given more than they can handle for their age.[239] Children who are disobedient should be administered greater attention, instruction, discipline and caring.

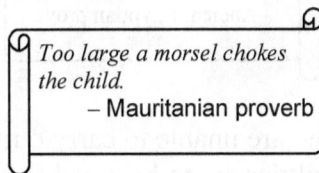

> *Too large a morsel chokes the child.*
> – Mauritanian proverb

1.3. Adults who fail or are unable to meet their responsibilities to their children should be admonished as to the nature of the violation. They are to be assisted by the community with counseling[240] in learning skills for coping and conflict resolution within the family and or training in household as well as practical work skills for making a living; also other members may be assigned to assist them to work towards meeting their responsibilities.

> *Advise and counsel him; if he does not listen, let adversity teach him.*
> -Ethiopia proverb

1.3.1. Meeting the responsibilities of caring implies non-violence. Those who speak violent words are to be issued a warning and counseling for anger[241] issues and should be instructed in conflict resolution skills. Those who commit physical violence are to be physically detained and counseled and if necessary segregated from the society until they are able to be rehabilitated and reintegrated. The failure to accept this regulation leads to expulsion from the society and referral to the greater social authorities [police, courts].

> *I have not allowed myself to become angry without cause.*
> –Ancient Egyptian proverb

1.4. Elders who are unable to carry out their social responsibilities are to be cared for and made comfortable by the society.

1.4.1.1. Those elders who are able but unwilling to fulfill their role in society are to be admonished by the Village Council and assigned assistance from other family members or members appointed by the society to help them work through the problems they may have.

140

1.4.1.2.If an admonishment and counseling fail to resolve the issue the elder should receive a warning from the Council.

1.4.1.3.If a warning fails the elder should be made comfortable but not allowed to interfere with the otherwise balanced and ordered society.

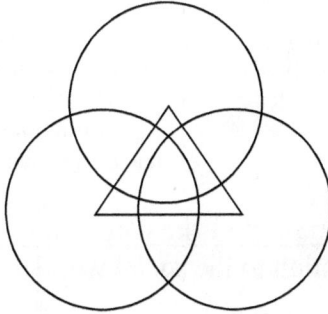

# Regulations in the area of village

This section presents an outline of essential regulations {laws, rules, guidelines} of village {community} based on the responsibilities to village for anyone who wants to create or sustain a society based on *African Proverbial Wisdom Teachings*.

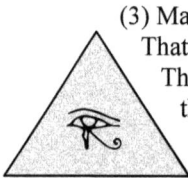

(3) May you be justified before The God,
That a man may say of you even when you are absent,
That you punish in accordance [with what is just for the crime].

-Instructions to Meri-Ka-Ra
[Ancient Egyptian Wisdom Texts]

2. **Regulations based on the Concept of village** - The human in relation to the social world.

As stated earlier, if a society is constituted in such a format that prevents people from acquiring the necessary opportunities for advancing themselves and or providing for their needs then that society is not operating in accordance with the African ethic of village (Community) and should be corrected. A society may be impaired by the greed of individuals or groups within the society, or by other societies that are interfering with the righteous development of the other society, or by ignorance (distorted societal philosophy).

2.1. the violation of the regulation to care for the village and not just for the family, displaying greed, hoarding resources, unwillingness to share[242] with others and contribute to the common good should be confronted by:

> *Knowledge is like a garden:*
> *if it is not cultivated, it*
> *cannot be harvested.*
> -Cameroon proverb

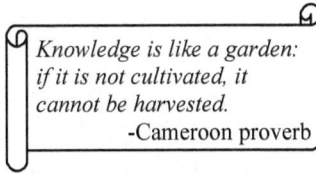

2.1.1. The violator is issued an admonishment and counseling. Councilors may make further recommendations to resolve the situation.

2.1.2. If an admonishment and counseling fail to rectify the situation:

2.1.2.1. The Council will issue a warning and offer solutions to resolve the problems, promote order and balance in society and may take other action such as ordering the violator to stop their activities that are in violation of the village regulations.

2.1.3. If the warning and solutions fail to resolve the issues due to the unwillingness of the violator(s) to comply with these regulations and or the directives of the council, the council may take other actions to resolve the problem including expulsion of the violator(s) from the society.

2.1.4. It is the responsibility of the council and village to produce regulations that promote the spirit and meaning of the Fundamental African Ethical Conceptualizations.

2.1.4.1. If the regulations of the council and or village elders are found to violate the ideal of promoting peace, harmony and advancement in the African society those regulations are to be reviewed and changed in order to reflect the spirit and meaning of the conceptualizations.

2.1.5.  Serious breaches of the ethical code such as stealing, fraud, physical violence, criminal behavior and any other action that the Council determines to be a serious infraction will be cause for expulsion and notification to the appropriate civil [legal] authorities.

2.1.6.  In the event that a Leader or Council member of the African society should become physically or mentally incapacitated and become unable to fulfill their role and duties they may be removed from their positions.

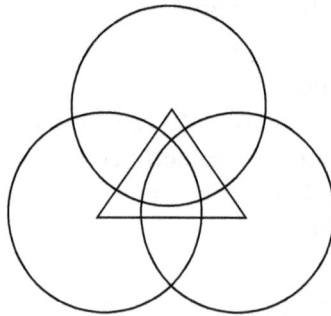

# Regulations in the area of Spirit

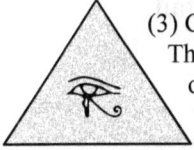

(3) Good nature allows a man to experience heaven,
The cursing of the [angry and agitated ones] is painful to
oneself.

-Instructions to Meri-Ka-Ra
[Ancient Egyptian Wisdom Texts]

This section presents an outline of essential regulations {injunctions, guidelines, admonitions} for a proper relationship with Spirit based on the responsibilities to Spirit for anyone who wants to create or sustain a society based on *African Proverbial Wisdom Teachings*.

3. **Regulations based on the Concept of connection to the Universal Divine** -that expresses as all nature and transcendental of nature - The human in relation to the spiritual world.

> *A man with too much ambition cannot sleep in peace.* - Baguirmi proverb

3.1. From a communal point of view, a society is responsible for providing an environment that is conducive for spiritual evolution. This is accomplished through the government and social institutions that are setup to meet the needs of people instead of facilitating the establishment and maintenance of social classes, plutocracies or oligarchies. According to African Proverbial Wisdom Teachings, the leaders of the society are charged with the responsibility of taking actions that uphold this highest of social ethics for the common good. Their ambitions cannot overtake their desire to serve[243] and pursue wisdom for if those in leadership are not wise enough to be an example of peace and harmony and teach[244] their people the wisdom of ethics and lead them to proper ethics, that society will ultimately fail.[245]

> *He who learns, teaches.*
> -Ethiopia proverb

3.2. The practice of religious ritual is for the purpose of "making peace" with the spirit. That is, promoting harmony between human life and spirit essence. This is the concept behind the Ancient Egyptian hieroglyphic symbol known as *htp* or *Hotep* or *Hetep.* This relationship between the human and the spirit is better thought of as a relationship between soul and Spirit. In order to discover the spirit a human being needs to find peace in life and it has been discovered that fulfilling the HTP responsibilities of life and the cultivation of proper relationships allows the personality to discover peace with the world. Through that peace, the egoism and neuroses of the personality, expressing through dualities, worries, anxieties, desires, frustrations, etc., subsides and it is then possible, through altruism, goodwill and contentment, to discover the ever-present and all-encompassing Spirit within and all around. The soul is the individual human being's spirit essence, a relationship not unlike that between a drop of water and the ocean. The individual soul is the drop of water and the Spirit is the ocean. The universal "Spirit" means the consciousness pervading all Creation, like all the water in all the oceans. The individual has a 'drop' of conscious awareness while the Spirit is all-encompassing

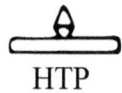

consciousness pervading the Creation. This is an essential process of society that promotes harmony between not only human beings and spirit but also between human beings and the family and the society and The Spirit.[246] The same Spirit is where the individual souls of all living beings arises from and is what they are connected to. Therefore all souls are connected through Spirit and inspirit all are one.

> *Then they all fall over onto their backs assenting by clapping their hands and saying, "Be appeased, be appeased."*
>
> -Tonga proverb

3.3. The elders in a society and a family are responsible for disseminating the mythic teaching of the society to the young. Myth is a language that includes the story of the society and humanity, the place of its members in the order of the society and, in the greater scheme of things, the place of the society in the world and the cosmos. A myth relates the individual to their higher nature and informs of the realms beyond the physical plane. It provides meaning to one's existence and purpose to life and instructs the individuals of a society as to the goals of life in the realm of the living and the realm of the afterlife.

3.4. An individual is responsible for accepting the myth, listening to its teaching, reflecting upon its meaning and applying it in life thereby developing ethical conscience and personal purity in order to promote peace with the world and brightness of intellect so as to understand the deeper wisdom of the mythic teaching.[247]

3.4.1. The proper application of the mythic teaching and philosophy leads to metaphysical experiences and intuitional realizations that allow a human being to experience the wisdom told in the mythic and proverbial teachings, thereby confirming the existence and presence of Spirit in higher consciousness. This also produces not just wise but enlightened elders, spiritual leaders and enlightened ancestors.[248]

𓀀𓄿𓎡𓅱𓏛𓏥 *Akhu,* "enlightenment" and 𓊪𓀭𓈖𓏏𓀭 *Sheps-* "nobility, honor, venerable-ness, honored ancestors."

3.5. If these regulations are not maintained a society becomes spiritually bankrupt and socially bereft of reason for its existence. It may devolve into secular goals of life that are destructive, selfish, petty and vile. Such a society loses its spiritual conscience and awareness of the essential divine nature of life, human beings and nature itself. In such a society great crimes, hedonism, devastations of nature and personal degradations are possible. In modern times the supervision of this issue is the paramount responsibility of the Village Council, President, Chief, Prime Minister, in other words, the leadership of the society regardless of whatever format of leadership is used.

> *If your house is burning, there is not time to go hunting.*
> - West Africa proverb

3.5.1. The council recognizes that human beings have three essential needs, *food, shelter and opportunity*[249] {opportunity for self actualization in society and self-realization in spiritual life}; if these needs are provided for there is a greater possibility for maintaining a well ordered, peaceful and harmonious society that respects humanity, sustains nature, truth and spiritual conscience for those currently alive and those who will come in the future.[250]

3.5.2. Conversely, if the basic needs of life are not provided, the higher ethical dimensions of the personality are more difficult to develop. So priorities[251] are understood in African ethics but this does not mean that ethics can be discarded or allowed to be forgotten in times of crisis since such an eventuality would lead not only to the physical degradation of the society but also to the ethical, moral and spiritual degradations as well.[252]

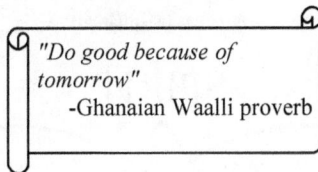

> *"Do good because of tomorrow"*
> -Ghanaian Waalli proverb

3.6. The council has the responsibility to use the Fundamental Principles of African Ethics, the Triune concepts of African socio-spiritual ethics as guidelines for creating further regulations as necessary.

3.6.1. The Fundamental Principles of African Ethics, the Triune concepts of African socio-spiritual ethics may not be changed by the present or future council members since these are transcendental principles that apply to all societies and in all times of history.

3.6.2. However, the regulations related to the transcendental principles and the manner of their implementation may vary with time.

3.6.2.1. In varying degrees of application and enforcement depending on the level of human evolution but may not be altered, as they represent timeless socio-spiritual constants that reflect human and cosmic truths that do not change with time [the manner of their application may need to be adjusted depending on the time in history].

**Figure 211: The Architecture of African Proverbial Wisdom Teachings: Combining the Blueprints, Part 2- Putting it all together-The Blueprint Components for an Architecture of Civilization**

The Blueprint Elements for an Architecture of *African Proverbial Wisdom Teachings* is a scheme in which all of the components of a well ordered society come together, as layers or constituent parts (organs, limbs, etc.) of an organism, to promote the creation and sustenance of a real and viable and sustainable civilization (a living healthy body) as opposed to a society based on a culture of barbarism, vulture-like dependency on other societies and the destruction of the environment. The Blueprint Elements for an Architecture of African Proverbial Wisdom Teachings is designed for a True Society Based in Wholistic and Fulfilling Human relations, Responsibilities and Regulations for Success in Family, Community and Spiritual Enlightenment.

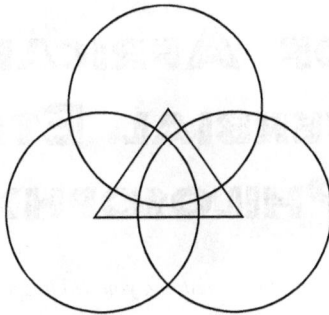

# CHAPTER 5
# IMPLICATIONS FOR MODERN PROFESSIONALS, GOVERNMENT AND RELIGIOUS LEADERS BASED ON THE CONCEPTUALIZATIONS OF AFRICAN PROVERBIAL ETHICAL PHILOSOPHY

*If you don't stand for something, you will fall for something.*

- Africa proverb

# Ethics and Professionalism VS. Expediency, Power and Greed in Society

**T**his section presents essential concerns for anyone who wants to create or sustain a viable and effective practice of ethical professionalism based on *African Proverbial Wisdom Teachings*. Throughout the history of governments and social orders perhaps no more important question can be asked than can the ethical professional find a place in today's society? The present condition of world politics would seem to be nothing more than the latest manifestation of Machiavellian political intrigue, what with all the wars, threats and fears that plague society; and when we examine many of the world's problems we find western governments and corporations, especially the United States and other western countries, but now also emerging powers such as China, supporting undemocratic governments, destabilizing governments, supporting torture and global economic swindling of poor under-developed countries while maintaining a high level of fear and greed in the populace. In that paradigm, ethics in government is treated by the power elite as a luxury that is not afforded by that which is expedient. And what is expedient is that which secures power and wealth quickly, not virtue. While there are many professionals in business and in government and perhaps even more in academia and the private sector, the expediency of politics demands the maintenance of power at all costs and the paradigm to be upheld and maintained is the Western way of life, which would seem to be based on Machiavelli's concept of maintenance of the position of the aristocrats, with any comforts given to the people being mere expenses in the cost of maintenance of the wealth, power and privilege of the aristocrats. In such a world what is ethical and how would a professional operate in such an environment?

Since it is such a central issue of African Proverbial Wisdom, let's look at the significance of ethics again and how it relates to modern culture and African Proverbial Wisdom. What are ethics? Ethics may be defined as a theory or a system of moral values.[253] Today's world condition was described by the words of Gregg

Easterbrook, author and lecturer and contributing editor at Newsweek and U.S. News & World Report as: "An ethic of service is at war with a craving for gain". Ethic has been recognized by many as meaning: the body of moral principles or values governing or distinctive of a particular culture or group and ethics are a system of moral principles as in: 'the ethics of a culture.'[254]

If ethics are a system of moral values[255] and if morality may be defined as concern with the distinction between good and evil or right and wrong and also the motivation based on ideas of right and wrong,[256] then we should consider that there are two ethics, that of right and that of wrong.

If ethics are a system of moral values and if morality may be defined as concern with the distinction between good and evil or right and wrong and also the motivation based on ideas of right and wrong, then we should consider that there are two ethics, that of right and that of wrong.

Conceivably then, within this context, the rightness or wrongness of an action is ascertained by the perspective from which it is determined. A gangster or a tyrant may consider murder as a 'good' thing while a priest may consider that 'bad. Yet the gangster may consider it bad if his or her gangster partner is killed while the priest may consider it good if a heathen or pagan were killed (to pave the way for conversions or the establishment of church power).[257] But the mother of either the priest or the gangster would consider it bad if their child were killed. Do not the lives of the priest and gangster have the same validity as those who were killed? Who's perspective is to be used in judging which life is less valuable or more worthy? In other words, who's ethics are correct and who's is wrong?

Both of the ethics described above are based on relative notions of morality based on subjective desires and varying degrees of humanistic understanding about the deeper nature of human existence {wisdom of the soul and Spirit-described above} and feeling towards the rest of humanity and the wider Creation.

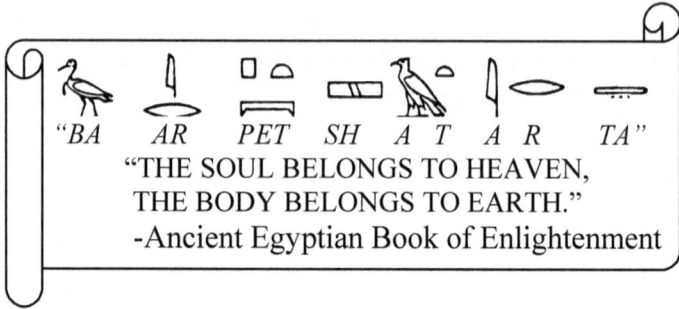

"BA    AR    PET    SH    A    T    A    R    TA"
"THE SOUL BELONGS TO HEAVEN,
THE BODY BELONGS TO EARTH."
-Ancient Egyptian Book of Enlightenment

So the invalidity [due to the relativity] of these subjective and morally relativist applications of ethics [the gangster ethic or the priest ethic], due to their lack of universal application, should mean that none are correct. What of the mother's ethics? If they would prefer to see others killed and not their sons their morals are relative and flawed. If they would not want to see their children or the children of other mothers be killed then their ethics transcend the morality of the priest and the morality of the gangster. What is it about the mother's ethics that allow it to transcend the others? The answer is that it has universality; in this context it is not subjective but objective as it represents the view of all mothers, who do not want their children to be killed. As the mother of all humanity the true ethicist rejects all relativist ethical theories and accepts only the ones with universal application because these transcend the relative nature of the personality and it's egoism.

Usually when the word morality is used it is thought of as a leaning towards what is righteous in terms of goodness, peace and harmony of the world, i.e. altruism. However, the definitions and circumstances presented above could allow the interpretation to go either way and presumably, the person making the determination of what is right or wrong would be the person or persons who have the power

156

to enforce their will. Here, that which is to be considered as the rightness of an action is determined by how effective it is in promoting the will of the actor, the perpetrator of the action; this is of course a self-serving evaluation, subjective and therefore invalid from an objective, higher, transcendental point of view. This of course, from an objective point of view, is a degraded development of ethics. Therefore, even in the definitions allowed by society, the very ideas of right and wrong can be considered as arbitrary or at best subjective. There is a danger also in conflating the ideal of ethics with morality when this is considered in association with particular religious tenets or egoistic social, parochial ideals, partisan political or economic objectives. Ethics would tend to look at a question in terms of rightness (correctness) or wrongness (incorrectness) while morality would tend to define it in terms of good or evil. If this theory could be applied it could perhaps be done by approaching others in terms of rightness or wrongness which implies the recognition that all have been right and wrong in the past and the wrongness or rightness of a person is separate from their human worth so all can learn and change and that through discussion and understanding the correct path may be discovered and followed by all. But even if there is no agreement the parties agree to disagree and not label each other as less than human or as less deserving of human respect; and each party allows the other to exist in peace to the extent that the actions of either do not harm the other.

However, throughout history, the application of moral standards by one person or group over another has seldom been equitable or compassionate. The egoistic and self-serving interests of individuals and or groups tends to win out over the altruistic aspects of the personality. The application of the relativist standard of good or evil implies that one party is absolutely correct and the other is incorrect and further, that one is bad and one is good; and from this arises the next logical self-serving ideal that the bad one should be destroyed while the good one should be preserved. In the presence of religious fanaticism which includes literalism and fundamentalism the morality degrades into irrational ideological adherence to religious tenets that, even though they may include easily provable false facts or concepts will be held onto and proclaimed by those who espouse them, as ideals for all to adopt, failing which those who do not adopt them should be destroyed since they are going to hell anyway so it does not matter what happens to them. Concomitantly, the acts of violence or other atrocities, against those others who fail to adopt the moral ideals, are excused since those who do not adopt the moral ideals are of less value than those who do; and of course those who do will be forgiven for committing the atrocities because they 'believe' in the ideals. This may be seen as an extreme and degraded condition but it is typical of many human beings throughout the world; and there are many who, though they do not agree wholeheartedly with the aforesaid, yet support those who do either through direct assistance or acquiescence. It does not apply only to morals in a religious context but also in the ethic of government and economics. One society may think it's form of government and or economics is superior and thus seeks to impose that on others. African Ethics, based on the ideal of *African Proverbial Wisdom Teachings,* promotes tolerance and understanding and the recognition of human freedom, which is after all a highly beneficial feature of human existence potentially for everyone, and particularly for those who can experience it because it allows them the psychological space to learn, reflect and consciously pursue self-improvement and fulfillment in life.

Considering religious morality, there is usually the tendency to consider it as what is good only, yet religions have committed atrocities and crimes, so while they have supposedly espoused what is good they have many times acted in accordance with what is bad for the people they hurt [since certainly the people who are hurt would regard the acts against them as bad even though the *ideological moralist*[258] might see such actions as good and beneficial to their own cause]. The church, mosque, temple (Christianity, Islam, Judaism) have also been party to political intrigues and have supported those who committed crimes. How then is a modern professional, basing their ethic on *African Proverbial Wisdom Teachings*, to carry on in a world where distinctions of ethics seem to be indeterminate and or relativist?

The ethic of one society may not be beneficial to other societies or to individuals within the same society. The work ethic or ethic of economics of one culture may dictate that some individuals of a society should work hard and get little pay while others get rich for doing little. Is this ethic good or bad and for whom? The work ethic or ethic of economics of one culture may dictate that the morals of the society are superior to that of others and therefore others should be subjugated or destroyed. Is this ethic good or bad and for whom?

In the context of this discussion on *African Proverbial Wisdom Teachings*, ethics are not dual but singular and not positive or negative but positive because they are not based or founded in the duality (egoism) of human existence but upon the universal concept of what is beneficial for family, community and spirit relations, in other words, for all and not just the individual. Therefore, anything thought to be associated with the African social ethic ideal, from the perspective of *African Proverbial Wisdom Teachings*, cannot be considered as an "African social ethic" if it is not beneficial, which also means that it promotes positive ethical conscience for all and tolerance and understanding and forgiveness for all; therefore, the "African social ethic" is also universal in scope, which precludes arbitrariness and favoritism and thus also prohibits lack of consideration and injustice for others.

Now, in view of the aforesaid, what is professionalism? If we should define professionalism as the "professional status, methods, character, or standards"[259] of a person, then what is the direction of the professionalism? There are after all professional hit men, professional con artists, etc. Could it not be argued that killing efficiently is highly praised in this society? Soldiers killing in war, police killing in self-defense or simply to stop someone from stealing property, and even efficient mobsters are praised, especially in popular culture, for their prowess in killing efficiently but most importantly for getting away with the murder. Thugs and mobsters are often highly sought after speakers, they have movies or TV shows made of them and their families, they are highly paid authors and commentators on TV. Some neighborhoods in the United States have people who live by a code of survival of the fittest and killing others efficiently and professionally there is seen as a valuable capacity. Fascination with Jesse James or even earlier, with barbarians such as Caesar, Attila, Napoleon and others, has characterized the society of the and culture of the United States of America and other Western countries as well as the cultures they have influenced; those cultures have been enthralled with the mystique of criminals and their lifestyle or that of the powerful and rich. Killing Native Americans and un-trainable African runaway slaves and later, Mexicans (because Texas was taken from them) was highly praised. Of course, before the colonization of the Americas, the people in Europe indulged in frequent wars and society was beset with many forms of violence and suppression of the population by torture and fear, as Machiavelli illustrates. Today the proliferation of television shows such as "24", "CSI", "Law and Order" and a whole host of detective shows attest to the promotion of and fascination with crime, violence, murder and torture. We often wonder what forces are driving the world to its current state of unrest, inequity and strife and we do not realize that people's own desires, and ignorant fascinations are contributing factors. If the current state of affairs of the world is the result of the best intellectual capacity as well as the best ethics and moral ideals (leading government leaders of the world (those who are heads of the most powerful countries) often claim to have the moral high ground and the best minds) what can be said for those ideals? With such a wayward moral compass how are professionals supposed to know how to direct their lives?

In order to find the answers to these questions we should first redefine what professionalism should be. In accordance with the logical findings of philosophy, professionals should be regarded as "people who do their jobs in a professional manner, those who do their jobs in an efficient and qualitative fashion." But we are still left with the notion of what should be the direction and purpose of that professionalism.

It might be argued that any person, who has the capacity to rise to the level of being considered a professional in any arena, also has the capability to decide on what is right and wrong from an objective standpoint. However, that idea does not take into account the factor of the level of education and training in wisdom philosophy that the person may have or their upbringing, what their parents and the society expose them to, the propaganda that they receive from popular media and the government and a person's own desires and aspirations they bring with them into their life and pursue as they grow up. That experience colors a person's view of morality and professionalism because unless a person has engaged in intensive contemplation, philosophy and introspection, they are influenced by socialization as well as their own lower desires and neuroses. This brings up the question of nature versus nurture but eastern philosophers (from India and China) and southern philosophers (from Africa) would say it is not nature alone that wields influence over how a person sees life but also a person's inclination developed from previous lives, other wise known as (*ari* {Ancient Egypt} or *karma* {India}). Therefore, a person's morality and capacity for empathy, and compassion are not dependent only on instructions from society although they are strongly influenced by society. In other words, some people can be induced to perform certain actions or a person can rationalize their actions based on arguments that are in favor of or excuse those actions and or their own desire to engage in those actions {rationalization}.

But in the end it is the innermost reality of a person, their 'Higher Self', that dictates their propensity to express an altruistic ideal of morality. So, human beings may have a propensity towards ethics of egoism or ethics of altruism but how are those who have the propensity towards altruism supposed to understand, cultivate and follow their propitious path? This is where the *African Proverbial Wisdom Teachings* and their purveyors (griots, priests and priestesses, etc.) come in. Actually morality is not indeterminate except for those who are blinded or who blind themselves to the laws of nature since from the philosophy of the Taoists of China [the Tao] as well as that of the Vedantic sages of India [Dharma] and that of the Neterian Sages of Ancient Egypt [Ma'at] we learn that morality is an application of a cosmic constant based on the recognition that nature manifests order and balance and seeks to preserve life and provide for the good of all; failing the application of this natural law the universe imposes a movement to redress the imbalance, which may be considered as negative to the person who brought in the original imbalance by not following the directive from nature in the first place. Therefore, the study of nature provides an objective insight into ethics as opposed to the subjective relativistic ethics of egoistic human beings and their oftentimes self-serving laws and paradigms. This study is a primary subject of Traditional African Philosophy.

There are examples of ethical governments in history. Ethical government is one in which the professionals express the altruistic outlook of morality in their professional duties. Some notable examples of the highly ethical governments through history include Ancient Egypt up to the Asiatic invasions and India under Buddhist rule.

In modern times, some European countries are striving to promote ethical government and responsible social institutions that promote the welfare of the populace by providing a social safety network but neither the government nor individuals in those societies can become fabulously rich or powerful because the wealth is shared more evenly than in those countries that are strongly capitalistic, communist or secular in their outlook.[260]

In Asia there is the country called Bhutan, which was governed by a system of monarchy with a council, based on Buddhist traditions. Though recently the country has been moving towards western concepts, the most prominent policy and goal of the government of Bhutan is called "gross national happiness" as opposed to the western ideal of gross national product. In such societies the people are used to truth in government and they are used to getting people out of government who are not promoting the national welfare, but rather the initial tendency is to promote the common good because that is embedded in the culture itself. In cultures wherein the ideal is self-interest and profit above the common good, the positive ethical professional would have a difficult time succeeding. Entering into the corporate or governmental sectors is entering into a cauldron of excessive pressure to conform to the values of the pleasure seeking, power hungry, greedy philosophy. They might be marginalized if not ostracized and they would be relegated to promoting their ethics in their own circles and such circles would be regarded in the mass media and government as inconsequential or amusing curiosities. Countries such as Bhutan are considered as incomprehensible by most western onlookers but yet there are some of those who misunderstand or ridicule who may experience an unconscious longing. They are longing deep down for peace and harmony but they have invested so much in their understanding of the world and what should be pursued through the egoistic paradigm as the proper values in life that they cannot help agreeing with the ridiculers (the ideological moralists).

163

There is an Ancient Egyptian saying that goes: *"Virtues fail that are frustrated by passion at every turn."* In this way, people's own desires thwart their movements towards virtue and the world is eager to facilitate the pursuit of [but not abiding attainment] pleasures of all kinds and this ideal is "enshrined" in the United States declaration of independence where it states "We hold these truths to be self-evident, that all men are created equal, that they are endowed by their Creator with certain unalienable Rights, that among these are Life, Liberty and the pursuit of Happiness." In the aforementioned ideal, the optimal moral value is the pursuit of happiness in terms that are adjudicated by the individual and not the ideal based on an objective universal standard of happiness that may be defined as discovering the "Way of Nature" and harmonizing with it or promoting the welfare of all in social terms as providing the necessities of life and opportunities for advancement to all and in human spiritual terms as fulfillment of life's goals in relation to family, community and spirit. The altruistic values indeed conflict with the individual or corporate pursuits which are based on commercial, profit-making goals in view of the fact that hoarding necessarily deprives some segments of the population from acquiring sometimes even the basic sustenance needs for life. The moral relativism of those who espouse philosophies such as communism or free market economics is evident in that their stated goal is to promote what is beneficial for all and they may point to achievements such as the development of western countries. Yet they fail to explain how such development would have been possible without the exploitation of native peoples, African slavery and the despoiling of the earth through over-consumption and the production of pollution. They also fail to explain why the developments in those countries led to ever increasing disparities between a minority of rich and powerful people and the poor masses and the ensuing problems and sufferings of poverty on the majority of the population.

164

While some programs that are allowed to be carried to fruition, by governments or even the United Nations are beneficial to certain segments of humanity, such as relief efforts during a famine or after a natural disaster, none are fully empowering, liberating or edifying for the people they are supposed to help, presumably for the reasons outlined by Machiavelli, so that they remain docile and do not challenge the leader, as Machiavelli called him, "the Prince" (Presidents, Kings, Dictators, etc.). This ideal is implemented through central financial institutions such as the Central Bank, International Monetary fund, World Bank, etc. that maintain people in an indebted condition, backed by coercion of a segment of the population (middle class) and enforced by police and military forces. An example of the implementation of this policy is the propagation and maintenance of inflation, which robs the value of money (and huts the poor most).[261] Another example of such a policy is usurious loans to developing governments that end up keeping them poor and beholding the rich developed countries. An additional policy is referred to as "worker insecurity", an important policy maintained by the central bank of the USA (Federal Reserve) to control workers and force them to accept low wages to maintain them in a lower economic status as well as protect the power and profits of business owners by causing workers to be fearful about losing their jobs and thus docile and willing to accept subsistence level wages.[262] Therefore, in such an environment [collusion between government and business leaders to exploit the masses {fascism}], the ethical professional is relegated to a secondary position [since they do not agree with nor cooperate with the corruption of the current prevailing government and business communities] in which virtuous works or projects may exist as propaganda pieces {ineffective due to poor funding but useful to give the appearance of altruism and goodwill}, or if they serve the purpose of the power elite to ingratiate to the masses for political support during campaign times or if it does not interfere with the designs of the power elite for obtaining more material wealth.

So, in conclusion, the altruistic ethical professional needs to be concerned with not only how to promote that which is good for society but also how to support there own needs both material and spiritual, so that they may find the fortitude to work for the good of humanity despite their lack of support by the establishment (government and business institutions). The ethical professional should seek to join with other ethical professionals in order to support each other and coordinate and make their efforts more effective. We might see the ethical professional as the voice of reason that remains after the cacophony of war has temporarily silenced. In that silence some good proposals are made and good government may be partially attained until the population forgets the wisdom of having ethical government and businesses, becomes greedy and bent on consumption and the power elite reach for more power and wealth once again. What little of the good works that may remain from previous times might be remembered after the next conflict, and so society trudges along on a desperate and slow pace towards the abiding peace it seeks but might never abidingly achieve.

In a higher sense the altruistic ethical professional is a person whose capacity for caring rises beyond the self and family but encompasses community and the world. The challenge, to find a way to care for all, is what philosophers of old have spoken about in many ways, the Christian ideal of caring for others, the Hindu teaching of Dharma, the Buddhist teaching of Dhamma, the Confucian concept of ethics, the Taoist teaching of virtue and the Neterian teaching of Maat (Spiritual ethics in society, religion and government) all point to the natural imperative to move towards virtue, harmony and peace. The struggle of life exists to provide the altruistic ethical professional and those who desire to become altruistic ethical professionals the opportunity to choose the path of virtue and through their actions exemplify the principles of altruistic ethical professionalism and in so doing discover the meaning and purpose of life and at the same time make the world a better place.

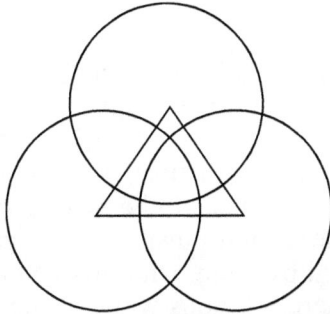

# Maat and Ubuntu Philosophy of Africa, Humanism and Humanitarianism in Present Day African Ethical Practice

263

**E**specially after Vatican II conference in 1964, after decades of denigration and attempts to convert African peoples, the Catholic church recognized African religion as a distinct and legitimate form of spirituality which continues to be practiced by a substantial number of people in and outside of Africa. In the present day, it is practiced by many who on one hand profess to be converts to Western religions while at the same time retain the practice of some aspects of African religion in their life. One reason for its persistence is the quality of *Humanism* that characterizes it and the recognition that all human beings have the same source and spiritual essence. Yet, African Philosophy, as an existing and distinct, viable contribution to humanity, as a system of thought and understanding, has not received such recognition among scholars in the philosophical studies disciplines. In this context we may think of Western Philosophy coming from Europe, Eastern Philosophy, coming primarily from India, and China, and Southern Philosophy which comes out of Africa. However, there is a difference between the Western ideal or understanding of religious eschatology just as there is a difference between the Western ideal or understanding of humanism and the African.

In Western understanding, Humanism has been defined as:

> *"**Humanism**", a philosophical viewpoint that stresses human reason as a source of authority and strives for human good in the present world. Humanist ideas can be found*

*from ancient to modern times, but the flowering of humanism came during the Renaissance.*[264]

In terms of African culture and society, humanism is not a determination about how people should be treated only using reason but may be further defined as: *any system or mode of thought or action in which human interests, values, and dignity predominate*[265] and not as: *Philosophy, a variety of ethical theory and practice that emphasizes reason, scientific inquiry, and human fulfillment in the natural world and often rejects the importance of belief in God.*[266] So, a distinction should be made between Western humanism and African humanism. African humanism can be detected throughout Africa both in ancient and modern times under the names Maat or Ubuntu or other names. It is of course present in *African Proverbial Wisdom Teachings.*

Therefore, because of this special feature of African culture, *African Humanism,* virtually all human expressions of the innate desire for spiritual discovery are allowed; in African religious practice other religions or religious practices have been welcomed due to this feature of African culture, its ability to accept and *absorb* the beliefs and practices of other peoples. There are some benefits and disadvantages to this feature. As an advantage a society could gain wisdom from the knowledge or practices of others but as a negative, they may adopt some harmful features of other societies that could be destructive and cause African culture to lose its identity, traditions, believe systems and wisdom, thereby causing it to be diluted, misdirected and thus deteriorate. This problem has been particularly evident during the period of colonialism and neo-colonialism, where the absorptive process occurred not under healthy conditions but diseased conditions. A healthy condition would be where two cultures, with their leaders, languages, traditions, etc. are active and intact, meet and exchange ideas. In the situation where African leaders have been decimated, replaced with incompetent or tyrannical leaders or completely eradicated the leadership and the people are forced to adopt different languages, traditions, and are suffering the ravages of slavery, racism, devastation of their social institutions, poverty and disease and then the people are introduced to alien religions, economic systems, customs and rituals, those people cannot evaluate these elements of culture with a proper conscience using their own culture and traditions as a foundation and benchmark for what cultural interactions should be and what the meaning of the other culture should have in their own context based on their own traditional wisdom.

**Figure 222: Maat-Ubuntu Philosophy throughout Africa**

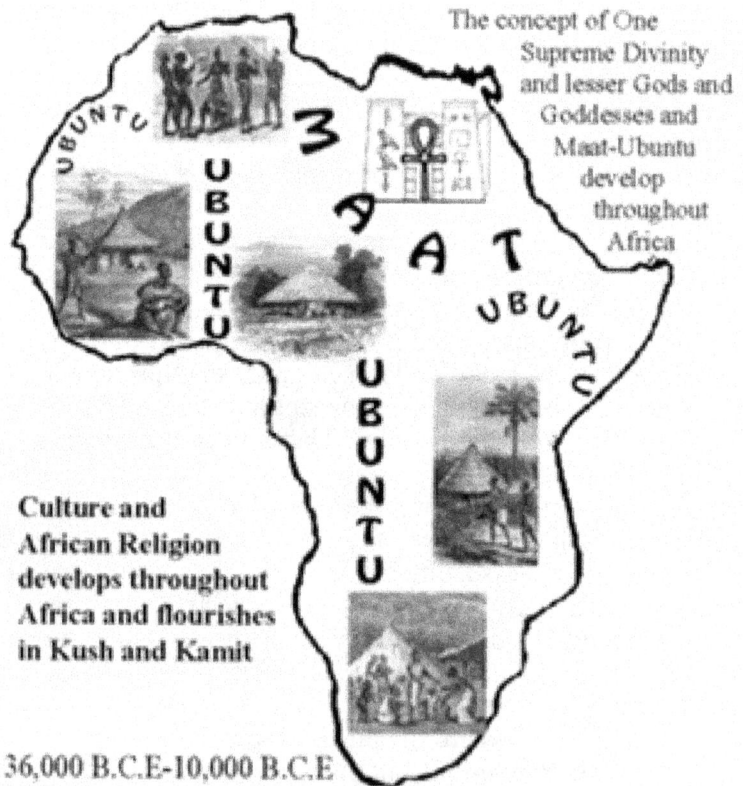

The concept of One Supreme Divinity and lesser Gods and Goddesses and Maat-Ubuntu develop throughout Africa

Culture and African Religion develops throughout Africa and flourishes in Kush and Kamit

36,000 B.C.E-10,000 B.C.E

The African term *Ubuntu* means humanism. Humanism is a fundamental concern for the human condition, a caring for fellow human beings with respect to their well being, but also it means a kind of openness, hospitality and compassion for those in need. The quality of Ubuntu, in Africa, has had the effect of tempering the harshness of other religions, as well as bringing to the forefront the sufferings and needs of others, and sometimes the inequities that are endured by others. Ubuntu is a kind of empathy and sympathy for others and a heartfelt desire to share with others. One important example of the effect of African religion and its quality of Ubuntu is the Aldura Church of Yoruba. In this church the Christian emphasis on salvation has given way to an approach that is more in line with the needs of the people, who grew up in a society that originated in traditional culture that was affected by many social disruptions [war, colonialism, disease, etc.] that had weakened it. Thus, the alien philosophy (in this case Christianity) has been altered, adjusted in some ways, though not completely; this process has been referred to as the "Africanization" of the religion. The priests function as diviners, healers and ritual leaders. The concept of humanism, in the African context, may be best expressed by the following quotations:

> "African belief is basically the humanistic belief that doing good is good, while doing anything bad is bad. You are rewarded here on earth for your good deeds and punished for your iniquities. Indeed, many Africans believe that the ultimate punishment for bad or iniquitous behaviour is death."

> -N. Adu Kwabena-Essem is a freelance journalist, based in Accra, Ghana

> "You know when it is there, and it is obvious when it is absent. It has to do with what it means to be truly human, it refers to gentleness, to compassion, to hospitality, to openness to others, to vulnerability, to being available for others and to know that you are bound up with them in the bundle of life, for a person is only a person through other persons."

> -South Africa's Archbishop Desmond Tutu, winner of the Nobel Prize 1984

When compared to the modern concept of Ubuntu, the ancient African Kemetic (Kamitan (Ancient Egyptian - 3,000 B.C.E. to 500 C.E.)) concept of Ari Maat (Maatian Actions) is found to be compatible with the Ubuntu concept of humanism or social awareness and caring. Maat is a philosophy, a spiritual symbol as well as a cosmic energy or force which pervades the entire universe. Maat is the path to promoting world order, justice, righteousness, correctness, harmony and peace. Maat is also the path that represents wisdom and spiritual awakening through balance and equanimity, as well as righteous living and selfless service to humanity. So Maat encompasses certain disciplines of right action which promote purity of heart and balance of mind. Maat is represented as a goddess with a feather held to the side of her head by a bandana and she is sometimes depicted with wings, a papyrus scepter in one hand and holding an ankh (symbol of life) in her other hand.

Forms of Goddess Maat

Maat should be though of as a philosophy, a goddess and also as a way of life. In Kamit (Ancient Egypt), the judges were initiated into the teachings of MAAT, for only when there is justice and fairness in society can there be an abiding harmony and peace. Harmony and peace are necessary for the pursuit of true happiness and inner fulfillment in life. Peace and order that are reached by force or injustice is not in accordance with Maat and such peace and order will deteriorate through ignorance and imbalance to unrest and chaos. Thus, Kamitan spirituality includes a discipline for social order and harmony not unlike Confucianism and Taoism of China or Dharma of India. Maat promotes social harmony and personal virtue which lead to spiritual enlightenment.[267]

Many people are aware of the 42 Laws or Precepts of Maat. They are declarations of purity (also known as *negative confessions)*, found in the Kamitan Book of Enlightenment (Egyptian Book of the Dead), which a person who has lived a life of righteousness can utter at the time of the great judgment after death. All of the precepts concern moral rectitude in all aspects of life which leads to social order. Order leads to prosperity and harmony for society and spiritual enlightenment for the individual.

In Chapter 125 of the Ancient Egyptian Book of the Dead, the fundamental principles of African Social Ethics are outlined where a person should be able to utter the declarations after living an ethical life:

> "I have done God's will. I have given bread
> to the hungry, water to the thirsty, clothes to
> the clotheless and a boat to those who were
> shipwrecked. I made the prescribed
> offerings to the gods and goddesses and I
> also made offerings in the temple to the
> glorious spirits. Therefore, protect me when
> I go to face The God."[268]

The teaching from Chapter 125 (above) is a reflection in the religious texts of the most basic Maatian principles for social order and human responsibility which are enumerated in the 42 Precepts of Maat and which are prerequisites for spiritual fulfillment in life. As an adjunct to the 42 precepts there are other injunctions given in the Wisdom Texts. The Ancient Egyptian Wisdom Texts form the foundation of Ancient Egyptian *African Proverbial Wisdom Teachings*. These in turn are elaborated in the tomb inscriptions of Ancient Egypt which are a class of scripture expounding on the teaching of the *PertmHeru* (Egyptian Book of the Dead) and the 42 Precepts of Maat. Central to this order and virtue are the acts of righteousness and the highest form of right action is selfless service. That is, all of the things a person can do to uphold truth, order and righteousness during their lives. These inscriptions provide insight into the nature of social ethics and their application, from the perspective of an Ancient African society which are applicable to present day life.[5]

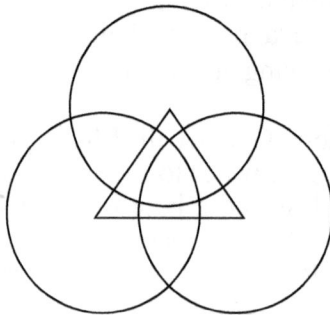

---

[5] For more on Maat Philosophy see the book *Introduction to Maat Philosophy* by Muata Ashby

# The Breakdown of African Ethics and the Plight of Native Peoples

The researcher Jarrod Diamond[269] postulated that up until recently in human history, the world's populations were about even as to their development in terms of their ability to wage war and control the environment. However, the nations of the Eurasian region were able to make use of technologies that allowed them to conquer other lands and peoples and gain control of the world before other nations could. In Diamond's view, the technological advantage, gained by taking discoveries from far off lands and ingeniously using those to construct war implements, is what spawned longstanding wars amongst European countries and led to the ideal of creating empires by dominating as many nations as possible. Some prime examples of the move to dominate other nations and create modern empires are the colonization of the "New World" (The Americas) and the "Scramble for Africa." History does not present non north Eurasian or Asiatic examples of megalomania.[270] In other words, in the tropical regions of the world there is no record in history of Alexander The Great-like, Caesar-like, Genghis Khan-like, Attila-the-Hun-like, or Napoleon-like personalities, or personalities that have exhibited the desire to extend their power and dominion to encompass the known world and or populations who would support such ideals and leaders who espouse such views.

There are several salient examples in world history that relate to the cultural aggressiveness of societies in the temperate zones of the world but since the peoples from the temperate regions of the earth have influenced the peoples of the tropics there have emerged examples in the tropics which are apparently influenced by the peoples of the temperate. In the past we have examples of empires and megalomaniac leaders who sought to dominate the world, like the ancient Greeks, the ancient Romans, Attila the Hun, Genghis Khan, the Ottoman Empire, the British Empire, and others. In the present day we have the American Empire. Presently, one prominent example of the move to dominate other peoples (imperialism) is the situation of the Israelis who oppress Palestinian peoples and occupy their lands. Another is the situation of the United States of America, together with some European countries, seeking to dominate and control other countries, like Iraq, Afghanistan, and several others.[271] In recent history we may consider examples from other ethnic groups around the world but as we are looking at African culture and wisdom we should look at examples in Africa that appear to follow the pattern of "inhumanity" characterized by the imperialist temperate zone culture of social dominance through war, economics or other means. In Africa, there is an interesting case of the "Bushmen" of Southern Africa.

The Bushmen (also known as Khwe (Khoe), Basarwa, or San) are peoples of South Africa and Botswana and Namibia, who live in the Kalahari. They have lived in southern Africa for at least some 20,000 years. The Bushmen, along with the pygmies of Central Africa, have been thought to be a possible source or root for the original female DNA lineage of Homo sapiens sapiens {human beings}—otherwise known as "Mitochondrial Eve", a female ancestor from which *ALL* human beings [Africans, Europeans, Asians, Native Americans, etc.] who are alive today, are descendants.

Traditionally the culture of the Bushmen has been of hunter-gatherer. The people lived in temporary wooden shelters. Even though the national constitution guarantees the people the right to live there in perpetuity, ever since the mid-1990s the central government of Botswana has been trying to move Bushmen out of the Central Kalahari Game Reserve, thus violating their rights. This is not unlike the situation faced by Native Americans, in what later became the United States of America, where the Natives were forcibly moved from their traditional lands to make way for new states and for the European population to usurp and develop for their own benefit. The Botswana government's position is that it is too costly to provide such basic services as medical care and schooling. It has banned hunting with guns in the Reserve and has said that the Bushmen threaten the Reserve's ecology. Others, however, claim that the government's intent is to clear the area for the lucrative tourist trade and for diamond mining. An important aspect, for our study is the issue of the differences in ethnicity between the Bushmen and the majority population that controls Botswana, the "Bantu."

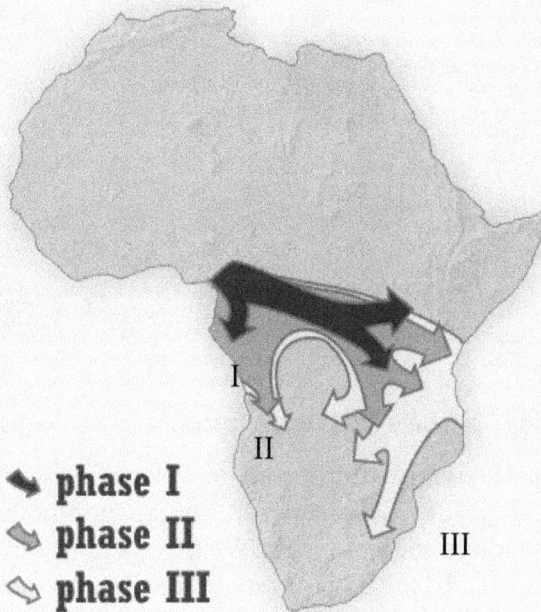

➤ phase I
➤ phase II
➤ phase III

**Figure 233: *Bantu expansion***

The term "Bantu" refers to over 400 different ethnic groups in Africa, from Cameroon to South Africa, united by a common language family, the Bantu languages, and in many cases common customs. "Black" South Africans were at times officially called "Bantus" by the 'white' apartheid regime. So the term Bantu was widely used as a term for the Bantu-speaking peoples in general. The term "Bushmen" was used to refer to the Khoisan or San people.

The scholarly consensus is that the Bantu speaking peoples of Africa were originally located generally in the area of present day Nigeria and then spread south throughout the area that was previously inhabited exclusively by the Khoisan [Bushmen] i.e. Southern Africa. The map below illustrates that expansion, which is believed to have occurred in three phases.

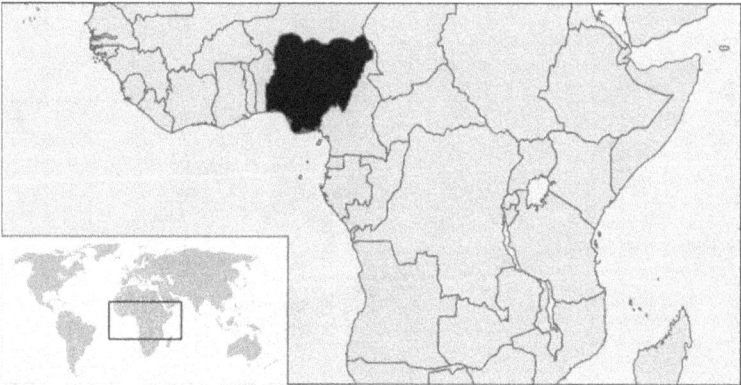

**Figure 244: Nigeria in West Africa**

Before the arrival of Europeans or Asians, perhaps due to the spread of the Sahara desert in the north, the Bantu expanded south and east from West Africa, in three major phases [I, II, III]. The Bantu expanded to encompass southern Africa but there was separation between themselves and the Bushmen due to their different cultures and traditions (ethnic backgrounds). To this day there is segregation as the two peoples hold separate values but also both of their respective cultures were affected by the ravages of racism that were imposed by European colonists. Today, the rift is wide enough to the extent that

the government of Botswana, now controlled by
descendants of the Bantu, after achieving liberation from
European [white] rule, actively imposes the similar kinds of
techniques on the Bushmen to dispossess them of their
lands as were used on them all [Bantu and Bushmen alike]
by the European colonists.

**Figure 255: San tribesman**

The Culture of the Bantu was different from that of the
Khoisan [Bushmen]. The Bantu people were not like the
Europeans, territorially minded. Instead, the Bantu culture
was group-related. Thus, they only observed the idea of
borders vaguely since there was plenty of land in Africa.
Borders were therefore not fixed. The Bantu acquired food
by means of agriculture and hunting primarily. The men

generally were responsible for hunting and women generally were responsible for agriculture.

**Figure 266: (Bantu) men from Nigeria**

As the Bantu population grew and as Europeans came in imposing imperialist ideals, and since the Khoisan people were primarily hunter-gatherers and so were more nomadic there developed problems between them and the Bantu and also the white Europeans. Sometimes other groups might move onto the lands that the Khoisan traditionally migrated from but returned to in different seasons so disputes over rights might arise. During the time of white rule in southern Africa the problems for the Bushmen were intensified as they were moved off valuable lands and attempts were made to dissipate their numbers not unlike what the government of the United States of America and other European colonial powers tried to do to the Native Americans in North and South and Central America as well as the Caribbean. After the end of white rule they have continued to be marginalized and their rights trampled by the descendants of the Bantu.

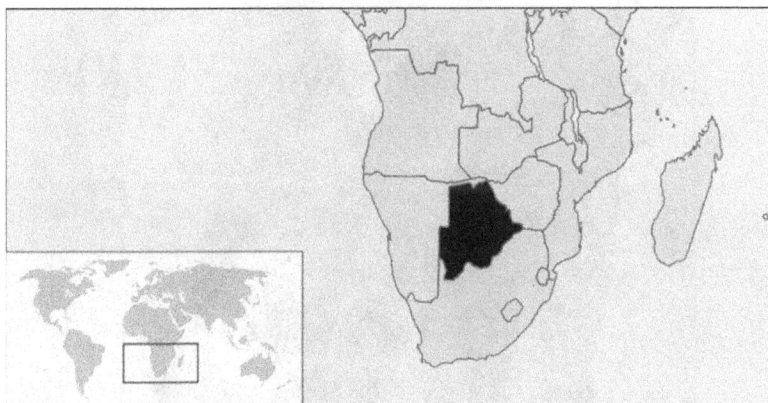

**Figure 277: Botswana in southern Africa**

Now, we may also consider an example from outside of Africa. On the island of Dominica, an example of freed slaves mistreating the pre-Columbian native population is found in the Commonwealth of Dominica [more popularly known as Dominica]. Dominica, not to be confused with the Dominican Republic, is an island nation in the Caribbean Sea. Dominica was first sighted by Christopher Columbus, and other Europeans in 1493 ACE. There they encountered the Caribs, the indigenous peoples [Native Americans].

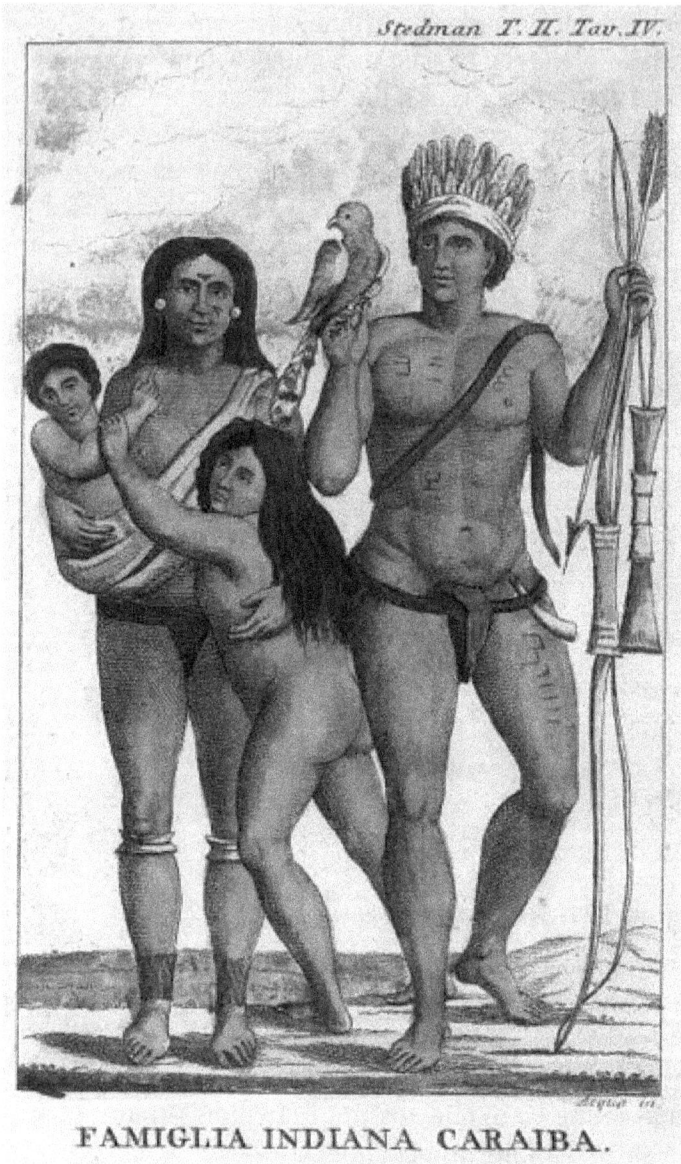

**Figure 288: Carib family (by John Gabriel Stedman)**

**Figure 299: Location of Dominica in the Caribbean**

The Caribbean Sea was named after the ***Carib***, ***Island Carib*** or ***Kalinago*** people who live(d) in the Lesser Antilles islands. When the Europeans attempted to enslave the Caribs the Caribs fought them and defeated the Spaniards so the Spaniards left the island. In the year 1635 ACE the French claimed the island for themselves and then sent missionaries to the island in the hope of converting the Natives and thus make them more pliable to be dominated [using religion to produce people who would submit to the religious authorities who are controlled or in partnership with the secular leaders [Kings, Queens, Merchants, Slavers, Bankers, military, etc.], but the missionaries also were unable to loosen the control of Dominica by the Caribs. France later ceded possession of the island [even though they were not in control over Dominica] to England in 1763 ACE. The British set up a government and were more successful in making the island a colony in 1805 ACE but were unable to dislodge the Caribs. The British emancipation of African slaves, which occurred in 1834 A.C.E. led to Dominica becoming the first British colony in the Caribbean to have a Black-controlled legislature in the year 1838. The "Black-controlled legislature" did not include substantial participation of the Caribs and later, coming to the 20th century, the "Black" population [descendants of the former African slave population] has

183

further attempted to diminish the rights and marginalize the descendants of the Caribs who still live on a section of the island. Today they have a territory an a format similar to the Indian reserves of North America.

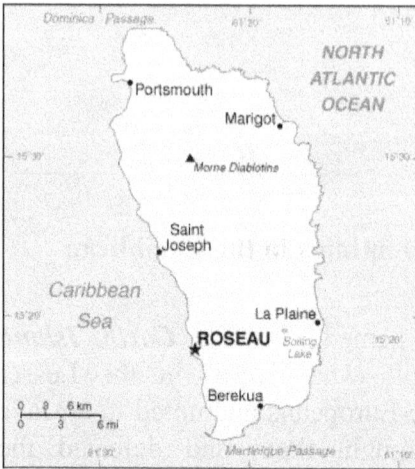

**Figure 30: Map of Dominica**

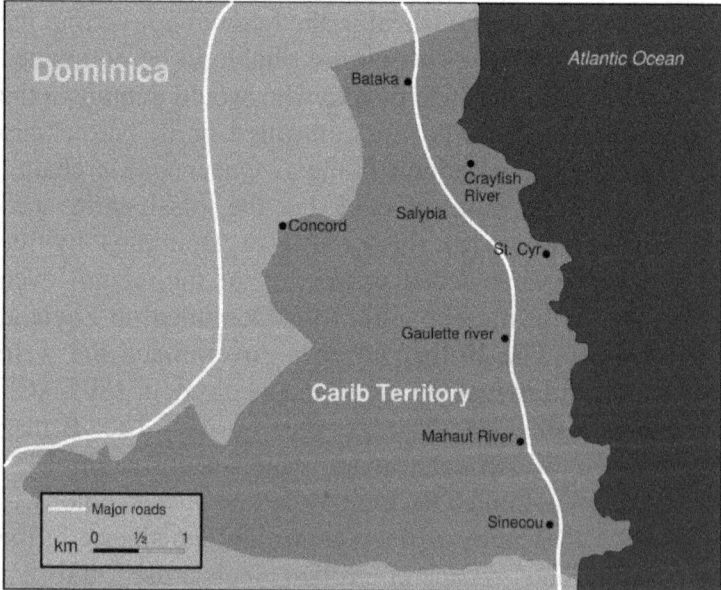

**Figure 301: Dominica's East coast territory of the Kalinago (tribe)**

The situation between Bantu Africans and the Bushmen Africans [Native Africans] in Africa and the situation between the descendants of freed African [Bantu Africans] slaves and the Native Americans in Dominica raises important human issues related to the age old question of nature versus nurture. If we are to accept, based on the solid evidence of examples throughout history, that the peoples of the temperate zones are more aggressive than those of the tropical zones how do we explain the fact that when the culture of peoples of the tropical zones are negatively affected by the aggressive segments of the populations of the peoples of the temperate zones [Europeans, Asians], and when the oppression from the peoples of the temperate zones is lifted, why is it that the oppression on the native populations [in the examples cited above: Khoisan or Caribs] is continued by the peoples of African descent who are now the dominant population? Why is it that, in many cases, the descendants of the people who were treated as slaves or who's culture was disrupted by European or Asiatic peoples, do not go back and restore their original cultures and traditions [societal philosophy, religion, language, etc.] but instead retain fundamental cultural features that were imposed on them by the oppressing cultures? Why is it that dictators and tyrants emerge in such populations even when the neo-colonial and post neo-colonial periods have passed?

**Figure 312: Dominican men playing drums**

We may observe firstly that the tyrants and dictators of Africa and the tyrants and dictators of South America (tropical zones), which were sponsored and kept in power by the western countries, cannot be considered as Alexander The Great-like, Caesar-like, Genghis Khan-like, Attila-the-Hun-like, or Napoleon-like personalities since those personalities attempted transnational conquests and megalomaniac attempts to rule the world and the actions of the tyrants of the tropical zones only affected their respective countries –even though their atrocities were egregious. Even if we consider the case of Shaka, of the Zulus, who is often referred to by European researchers, incorrectly as the "Napoleon of Africa", we do not find any transnational conquerors perpetrating wanton and wholesale destruction of countries and mass killings for the sake of a megalomaniac goal.

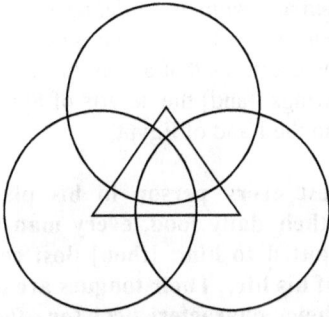

# African Proverbial Wisdom and the Revitalization of Panafricanist Movements

## One God, One Humanity, One Religious Ideal, One Spiritual Destiny: A Framework for Ecumenical African Spirituality

> One God, like whom there is no other. Thou didst create the earth by thy heart (or will), thou alone existing, men and women, cattle, beasts of every kind that are upon the earth, and that move upon feet (or legs), all the creatures that are in the sky and that fly with their wings, [and] the deserts of Syria and Kush (Nubia), and the Land of Egypt.

> **Thou settest every person in his place. Thou providest their daily food, every man having the portion allotted to him; [thou] dost compute the duration of his life. Their tongues are different in speech, their characteristics (or forms), and likewise their skins (in color), giving distinguishing marks to the dwellers in foreign lands... Thou makest the life of all remote lands.**
> -Ancient African-Kamitic (Egyptian) Hymn

The important verses above also mean that not only is there one God but that this being is the same God manifesting as the ultimate object of adorations in the varied ("different") religions of peoples who reside in foreign lands. Known in modern times as "pantheism" or the belief that there is one ultimate reality (God) behind all phenomena, this is a momentous realization which overshadows all attempts to characterize Ancient Egyptian-African spirituality and philosophy as primitive or idolatrous. This view expresses the understanding that Spirit transcends religion and that the particular religious manifestation is a product of the local culture but yet the same desire to discover the same Divine ultimate reality is

188

there in all the forms. This is not a divisive concept but an enlightened Panafrican perception of reality. This is the basic model upon which a modern understanding of religion and religious harmony can be promoted.

Further, God has created all peoples, all nations and countries and has appointed each person's country of residence, language and even their ethnicity and physical appearance or features. So all people, including those of foreign lands, have the same Creator and owe their continued existence to the same Divine Being.

The divisiveness due to differing religious views has been a continuing source of strife in the African community. Until this issue, is resolved the efforts towards African liberation and empowerment will continue to be frustrated. First and foremost we are spiritual beings, and so what is our common heritage as spiritual beings living as African people?

As it has been shown by our own scholars, Diop, Ashby, and others (including non-African scholars), that the world humanity, civilization and religion originated in Africa. Specific correlations have been discovered between the Nubian-Egyptian religion and the Yoruba, Dogon, Jewish, Christian, Islamic, Hindu, Buddhist, etc. faiths. Since the modern world religions and the spiritual traditions that developed from them have their roots in ancient African religion it therefore follows that any religious faith or spiritual organization that wishes to join the African Proverbial Wisdom based community needs to acknowledge the African origins of their faith and with this acknowledgement comes acceptance of other African based faiths the spiritual allegiance to the upliftment of African culture as a collective instead of remaining as fragmented people.

Since spirituality is the most important and therefore influential aspect of culture and since African culture is not one single monolithic body, but one composed of many elements with key points of commonality, it is important that the religious and secular leaders who want to consider themselves as part of the African Proverbial Wisdom based community outlined above should formally acknowledge these points and actively promote these in their individual congregations and independent functions. Otherwise a situation of downfall will inevitably occur, as have occurred several times in the past, which will erode the harmony of the community and disrupt the communal plan of action towards social upliftment. This problem is found exclusively when orthodox religions interact. Orthodox means adhering to a standard view which excludes all others. Orthodox religion is recognized as the leading source for most of the strife in the modern world because of the intolerant ideas and social environment that it foments. The problem or orthodoxy was not present in ancient times in Africa because traditional African religions (including Ancient Egyptian) were always ecumenical. Ecumenical means "of worldwide scope or applicability; universal." An ecumenical religion understands and accepts itself as an expression, among many, of the same ultimate spiritual reality and therefore it accepts other expressions by other people. The orthodox religion sees itself as THE only true and correct expression of spiritual concepts and religious practices. The orthodox view of spirituality was therefore not originally an African teaching, nor can it be said that such a concept is better than older traditional concepts developed in Africa because the traditional concepts worked for thousands of years prior to the introduction of orthodox religions into Africa. They worked in the sense that they allowed peoples of diverse backgrounds and spiritual traditions to coexist without destroying, enslaving or denigrating each other. Further, in countries outside of Africa where the orthodox religions are the main form of religion, these have led to more grievous conflicts including wars (civil and international) and atrocities, as well as the destruction of nature, than anywhere else or at any time in history. Moreover, such countries, basing their reasons on religion or racial superiority, were the originators and promoters of slavery, sexism and wars of conquest which in modern times continues to manifest in the form of "new world economic orders," hoarding of resources, male superiority, etc. So it is clear that countries with orthodox views of spirituality cannot claim to be more enlightened, benevolent or spiritual than those countries which espouse ecumenical, nature oriented, or mystical religions or ethical conscience as the basis for social order (African Proverbial Wisdom).

The council of an enlightened African community should not feel the necessity to compromise even one principle of righteousness and tradition to please any person. All adherents must sacrifice the orthodox and independent views for the sake of the community, the culture and the country (African Proverbial Wisdom based Community), for there is something greater than any religion and all people at some point know this. And if there is anything certain about African Spirituality is that it transcends culture and religion. Religion is a tool, and not an end in itself but a means to achieve it. Otherwise the practitioners of religion are following the Western paradigm of viewing their own tradition as the only true faith and this form of exceptionalism was never a part of African culture. African culture was always accommodating but not compromising of fundamental principles so it can no longer afford to accommodate people who bring in religions to Africa or to Africans which affirm the goals and aspirations of other peoples, cultures, governments or traditions which are not in the interest of African people, or Africa itself. Further, this means that people cannot be accepted into the African community simply because they are "black." Blackness is a description. Being African means more than color of the skin. It relates to conscience. So we have many people who exhibit varied hues and they can be African if they adhere to African principles. This is not a color issue therefore, but rather an issue of culture and spiritual consciousness. We

191

should not engage in or uphold the foreign concepts of racism or sexism. The precepts of righteousness are the standard of what is good or bad and these guidelines come from our own ancestors. Therefore, no modern leader or religion needs to establish the guidelines, since they are already there, just needing to be implemented again.

The African based movement should be founded in the Matrix of African Proverbs. This means it should also be led by a council and not just by individual leaders who live their lives based on worldly or non African principles of righteousness and ethical conscience.

**Council of Elders**

The council of elders is the traditional African system of leadership. They direct the society while upholding the traditions and customs that constitute culture. Culture is the glue of society which provides people with a sense of belonging and motivation to self-empowerment and freedom. The council of elders plan of organization was the traditional form of government in Africa, which led to its greatest success in ancient Kemet. It's purpose was to guide and protect the integrity of the social order and promote ethical and spiritual values of life for the whole society. Also, in ancient Kemet the council was made up of elders and not the young for reasons of maturity and wisdom. Further, in Kemet the council consisted of priests and priestesses in the earlier period and their removal and minimization led to the ultimate downfall of Kemetic culture. Many have asked me over the years, as they see the Africentric movement floundering and its adherents tiring of rhetoric, slogans, endless rallies and the failures of their leaders due to character flaws, what our movement requires at this time? Is it military strength? International organization? Reparations? Vast wealth? Land? Political power? How can any of these things help if a person is so degraded that he or she cannot effectively make use of them with wisdom and temperance? Further, what is the basis of the council? On what authority do the members direct society? They require more than history or old age. They need moral authority and this comes from having a spiritual basis in which all members of the community are seen as members of a family, instead of the culture of greed and individualism that separates and disintegrates. The council must work to make such a culture that is righteous, and which affirms the beauty and uplifting, peaceful and prosperous nature of African culture, so that people will not only want to be part of it but will feel desirous to not be left out of it. This cannot be achieved by being permissive and accommodating to those who contradict the altruistic principals since this would be an insult to the same ancestors whom we pour libations to. If we as elders are not ready to uphold these high principals then why should we be surprised to see the membership in Panafrican groups dwindling? Our people need more than slogans, marches, parades, music and dances. They need empowering real tools for self determination, self empowerment and self knowledge, and we should not be afraid to lose more adherents since these are disruptive elements and when we build something with a stronger foundation, others will recognize that the time for which they have waited has come and they will lend their support. Further, the children of today need to receive special attentions since they will not only be the future of society, but also the organization. So cultural events which transmit the higher ethics and philosophy to them are of extreme importance and urgency. This is because those events will have an even greater impact on them as opposed to the adults. These are some of the most important tasks of the council.

**Importance of the Philosophy of Righteousness**

*"There are two roads traveled by humankind,
those who seek to live MAAT and those who seek
to satisfy their animal passions."*
-Ancient African-Kamitic (Egyptian) Proverb

We need a foundation that is solid and then the house that is build will stand strong and not as previous movements which were stressing too much militarism, economics or political power as the means to the end. Freedom is not something to achieve, it is something to be. When one is free, one's thoughts, actions and appearance are automatically liberating. Spirituality is the key to liberating the person and a culture is made up of liberated people. So even if a people find themselves oppressed or enslaved physically they can remain free and thereby remove the yoke of oppression. Spirituality must be our primary basis and then all righteousness and prosperity will follow. Has this not been proven in our own story? Look at the history of Kemet, lasting for *thousands of years* versus other empires which lasted only centuries. Where is our high philosophy? The Chinese have Taoism and Confucianism, the Indians and Buddhists have Dharma. These philosophies have sustained those cultures through enslavement and wars. What happened to African philosophy? Capitalism and militarism are not philosophies, but political instruments. Philosophy is that which uplifts and enlightens and thereby strengthens. Leaders who talk culture but do not live it cannot develop the purity to live righteously or sustain their own convictions or that of their community and so they succumb to temptation, political cronyism, neocolonialism, disease, and a myopic vision of the goal of how to "determine the direction of civilization." The weakness of unrighteous living leads to a degraded culture and this degradation opens the door to ignorance, adversity, slavery and poverty of mind and soul. Providentially, the African legacy holds the keys to the question of how African society is to uplift itself. There has been much study of history and little application of its discoveries. Is the purpose to study African history and philosophy, natural health and spiritual enlightenment, so as to have an academic degree but continue to follow the popular culture of cancer causing hot dogs, coca cola, pizzas, prescription drugs, Hollywood distortions (like the mummy movies) and the fallacy of the Western way (capitalism which leads to economic prosperity for the few)? Further, many believe that the economic system of popular culture should be used to the advantage of the panafricanist agenda but are the panafricans to practice the economics of unrighteousness that had led to world economic disaster, the devastation of whole countries for their resources, the impoverishment of whole populations so that western countries may enjoy wealth and conveniences, wars that have killed millions so that western countries and their surrogates may remain in power, the rise of disease and cancer causing agents so that corporations may become rich by promoting processed and chemical laden foods, and not expect that they (panafricanists) will become diseased and in league with the unrighteous oppressors in the process?

A revival of the culture requires guidelines for order, justice and conflict resolution. In Kemet these were called Maat and Maat philosophy promotes social order and harmony so that the higher spiritual perspectives of life may be discovered. So we do not follow laws for the sake of just promoting harmony but for the higher purpose of promoting self-mastery, wisdom and human evolution. Maat is a social as well as spiritual philosophy on a same level as Taoism, Confucianism or Dharma. Why is it that so many talk about Maat and praise it but do not study or live it? Why is it that so many talk about the ancestors who professed the benefits of vegetarianism, virtue, abstaining from drugs and promiscuity, yoga, meditation, etc. and never study their teachings and of course never practice them? Yet they expect to lift the yoke of oppression and adversity. My suggestion is to work towards building the foundation that will compose the structure of the membership of an unassailable organization. Then the actions taken will be meaningful and effective. This is the hard road but the truer path to abiding freedom of the body, mind and soul. It seems to many that the spiritual path is selfish because people seclude themselves and do not "enjoy life." They consider that going to a party, drinking and sexuality followed by a hangover is real enjoyment. Yet it is only a temporary reprieve from the nine to five wasting of their great potential that they know is there deep down but which they also suppress through the varied distractions of life. These acts are the very ones, which weaken the body, mind and will. So is there any wonder why people cannot find the stamina and perseverance to succeed in the struggle towards establishing ethics and justice in the world? How can we have ethics and justice in the world if we do not live it as individuals, groups, societies, etc? This leads to the understanding of why apparently well meaning but still worldly leaders and their movements fail, because they are living in accordance with values and ideals of cultures other than that which is presented in the African Proverbial Wisdom Teachings. Specifically, how can a society succeed when it is living in accordance with values that are antithetical to it's purported ideals? Panafricanists who supposedly want to create a Panafrican social order cannot do so by living and supporting the cultures they live in that are not based on African Proverbial Wisdom. For example, a Panafrican leader who mainly uses non-African dress, eats non-African food, prays to nonAfrican gods and or goddesses, supports non-African values in economics, and other social areas cannot expect to see an African ideal emerge. This is the challenge that faces Panafricanists or anyone who is striving to live by the ideal of the Matrix of African Proverbs.

# EPILOG

**W**e may conclude that when a people's culture is damaged or destroyed, that people's future is in danger because culture is needed to give direction and a sense of purpose in life. Culture is not in the DNA or genetics of people; it needs to be continually learned and supported in order to be passed on to the next generation. Otherwise it can be lost. This applies to tropical as well as temperate zone peoples.

This process may be intensified when an alternative culture is introduced and artificially sustained among the previously peaceful and ordered population. Neocolonialism is a prime example of the sustenance of an artificial paradigm but one which can become, over time, the mainstay of a peoples cultural perspective, as the original culture is forgotten or otherwise corrupted. In this manner the culture of a people can be affected, even manipulated or changed completely by affecting (distorting, removing, replacing) the current cultural institutions (elders, teachers, customs and traditions). This process may be likened to grafting the cultural aspects of one culture onto that of another. Culture is not the absolute and ultimate determiner of a person's fate but it is the necessary infrastructure the personality needs to derive its sense of community, ethics and self-concept as a human being. This infrastructure is the basis for the process of personal and spiritual self-discovery. Therefore, it is possible to "re-program" people if their language, traditions, relationships etc. are taken away or replaced with other ideals. However, among some populations affected by colonialism and neo-colonialism, there are some signs that damaged culture is now being repaired to some extent, not necessarily in terms of returning to it's previous standard of cultural values but, in most cases, at least turning away from the culture of capitalism, classism, sexism, racism, imperialism and adopting more humanistic and humanitarian cultural values. South America has taken the lead through the recent political movements of the last eight years which have reached to the point that 80% of the people, who have not previously achieved the capacity to vote in non-rigged elections, have voted for political parties and movements that oppose the USA and European concept of hegemony and economic imperialism and have begun to form alliances between different countries to band together in the event that the USA makes any moves against them such as those which occurred in the second half of the 20th century [political assassinations, placing military dictators in power, subverting economies, etc.][272].

In Africa the liberation of South Africa, the freedom and prosperity of Botswana and the elections of new presidents in Ghana and in Liberia and other countries also point to post-neo-colonial signals of moving beyond alignment with western political controls. However, many examples throughout Africa can be seen where the colonial and neo-colonial rule [military imperialism] apparently was ended, but the economic controls [economic imperialism] remained in place [such as in the case of South Africa]. Yet, populations around the world are becoming wise to the tactics of the west of fomenting social, economic, and political disruption and destabilization by financially backing thugs or unscrupulous people [aristocracy, oligarchy] who want to have power and become rich by selling out the resources of the country to western countries for compensation to themselves while allowing the population at large to languish in poverty.

It is important to understand that the greatest and most powerful way to promote freedom from imperialism as well as promote internal prosperity, balance and order in a society, is to readopt the preexisting societal philosophy and implement it's cultural ideals that allowed the society to exist in balance and prosper before the disruption occurred. This is not to say that there can be no benefits derived from the imperialist culture, but those should be judged against the native, preexisting cultural values. In this way the culture may restore balance to the society and the individuals will benefit by growing up and living in a society where they would be able to fulfill their life goals and spiritual aspirations as opposed to living in an oppressed culture where values are corrupted, day to day life is a struggle to maintain virtue or even survive from one day to the next; in such a culture the struggle to meet the day to day necessities of life precludes the capacity to fulfill people's life goals and spiritual aspirations. It is exceedingly difficult to practice meditation or be altruistic while bullets are flying, political corruption is endemic, where crime is rampant or there is not enough food to eat, etc. So, such groups that successfully turn away from the imperialist cultural values will be less vulnerable to the designs of foreign controlling forces. If we consider Africa as being now in the position that most South American countries were in the 1970's, 1980's and early 1990's we could conclude that many African countries are lagging behind in their cultural and economic emancipation from the old colonial forces by a factor of 20-40 years.

Nevertheless, the point is that a culture devoid of a positive societal philosophy of life which promotes ethical human treatment can leave a society vulnerable to manipulation and exploitation. This can occur to people who live in the temperate as well as tropical zones of the world. The solution is to re-institute and maintain, through constant reinforcement and vigilance, the ideals of ethical culture so as to create, support and maintain a positive society that can have the possibility of developing into a civilization and not remain in a primitive state, susceptible to the control of others or perhaps even devolve into a debauched barbarous {imperialist} society regardless of the level of its technological advancement.

It is important to understand that, being composed of human beings, whose generations do not accumulate knowledge, but rather need to learn again and again, all human societies are susceptible to degradation if the wisdom of life is not imparted by responsible elders of society. Therefore, it is incumbent upon all who want to see a return to real and abiding human values that were discovered and practiced long ago, that created great civilizations that lasted for thousands of years, should endeavor to learn, practice and disseminate this wisdom to all levels of society. Then the legacy of the ancients and the benefits of the wisdom teaching will be effective for our times and for our posterity.[6]

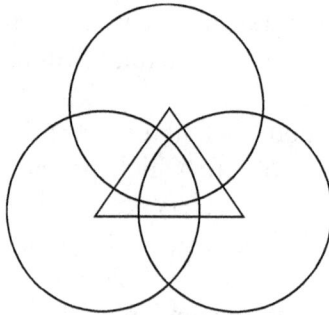

---

[6] For more on the study of Culture see the book *COMPARATIVE MYTHOLOGY* , *Cultural and Social Studies and The Cultural Category-Factor Correlation Method: A New Approach to Comparative Cultural, Religious and Mythological Studies* by Muata Ashby

# NOTES & AFRICAN
# PROVERB REFERENCES

[1] matrix. (n.d.). *Dictionary.com Unabridged (v 1.1)*. Retrieved April 10, 2009, from Dictionary.com website: http://dictionary.reference.com/browse/matrix

[2] The use of this term should not be taken by the reader as tacit agreement with the concept of race. It is used here merely as a description using a familiar term. The author does not subscribe to the idea of racial differences between human beings. There is only ONE *human race*. The dictionary definition of this term follows: mis·ceg·e·na·tion   Pronunciation[mi-sej-*uh*-ney-sh*uh* n, mis-i-j*uh*-] –noun

1. marriage or cohabitation between a man and woman of different races, esp., in the U.S., between a black and a white person.

2. interbreeding between members of different races.

3. the mixing or a mixture of races by interbreeding.

[Origin: irreg. < L *miscé(re)* to mix + *gen(us)* race, stock, species + -ATION; allegedly coined by U.S. journalist David Goodman Croly (1829–89) in a pamphlet published anonymously in 1864] miscegenation. (n.d.). *Dictionary.com Unabridged (v 1.1)*. Retrieved September 04, 2008, from Dictionary.com website: http://dictionary.reference.com/browse/miscegenation

[3] The use of the terms "black", "white", "brown", etc. is only descriptive of the appearance of people due to their development in certain geographical regions of the world [it has been demonstrated that geography affects the outer appearance of human beings]. The use of these terms in not a designation of racial types since there is only one human race.

[4] The term Mountains of the Moon or *Montes Lunae* referred to a mountain range in central Africa that was long believed to be the source of the White Nile.

[5] see the books: *African Origins of Civilization* and *The Black Ancient Egyptians* by Muata Ashby

[6] The use of the terms "black", "white", "brown", etc. is only descriptive of the appearance of people due to their development in certain geographical regions of the world [it has been demonstrated that geography affects the outer appearance of human beings]. The use of these terms in not a designation of racial types since there is only one human race.

[8] S. Gertrude Millin, *Rhodes*, London, 1933, p.138

[9] See the book *Collapse of Civilization* by Muata Ashby

[10] ibid

[11] "I spent 33 years and 4 months in active service as a member of our country's most agile military force--the Marine Corps. I served in all commissioned ranks from second lieutenant to Major General. And during that period I spent most of my time being a high-class muscle man for Big Business, for Wall Street and for the bankers. In short, I was a racketeer for capitalism. I suspected I was part

of a racket all the time. Now I am sure of it. Like all members of the military profession I never had an original thought until I left the service." -Major General Smedley Darlington Butler, USMC (1881 – 1940) Double recipient of the Congressional Medal of Honor. *War is a racket!* By Smedley Butler

[12] Kevin Shillington, History of Africa: Revised Second Edition, (New York: Macmillian Publishers Limited, 2005), 301

[13] A griot (pronounced /ɡɹi.əʊ/ in English or [gʁi.o] in French, with a silent t) or jeli (*djeli* or *djéli* in French spelling) is a West African poet, praise singer, and wandering musician, considered a repository of oral tradition. As such, they are sometimes also called bards.

[14] Context and Use Series Introduction Joshua N. Kudadjie, Series Editor of *TONGA PROVERBS FROM MALAWI* Copyright © 2001 by David K. Mphande

[15] proverb. (n.d.). *Dictionary.com Unabridged (v 1.1)*. Retrieved August 30, 2008, from Dictionary.com website: http://dictionary.reference.com/browse/proverb

[16] see he book *The Black Ancient Egyptians* by Muata Ashby

[17] see the book *Egyptian Proverbs* by Muata Ashby

[18] see the books: *African Origins of Civilization* and *The Black Ancient Egyptians* by Muata Ashby

[19] ibid

[20] ibid

[21] From the 1520s to the 1860s an estimated 11 to 12 million African men, women, and children were forcibly embarked on European vessels for a life of slavery in the Western Hemisphere. Many more Africans were captured or purchased in the interior of the continent but a large number died before reaching the coast. About 9 to 10 million Africans survived the Atlantic crossing to be purchased by planters and traders in the New World, where they worked principally as slave laborers in plantation economies requiring a large workforce. "Transatlantic Slave Trade," *Microsoft® Encarta® Africana.* © 1999 Microsoft Corporation. All rights reserved. Author's note: Other estimates run much higher but this one has been presented here to avoid needless arguments over the issue. Nevertheless this number pales in comparison to the deaths caused by the forced enslavement and kidnapping of Africans which estimates project at 100,000,000 (one hundred million) or more men, women and children.

[22] "Ethnicity and Identity in Africa: An Interpretation" *Microsoft® Encarta® Africana.* ©1999 Microsoft Corporation. All rights reserved.

[23] heathen. (n.d.). *Dictionary.com Unabridged (v 1.1)*. Retrieved April 19, 2009, from Dictionary.com website: http://dictionary.reference.com/browse/heathen

[24] the introduction of Hinduism to Africa is an interesting case, as the religion tends to be compatible with the indigenous religions of Africa, as both African and Hindu indigenous religious traditions are *henotheistic*. However, the culture of India, which includes notions of caste, that are practiced by many Hindus, tends to prevent full integration of Indian peoples with the peoples of other cultures, and also can lead to "racial" conflicts and tensions. see the book: *African Origins of Civilization* by Muata Ashby

[25] *Microsoft® Encarta® Africana.* ©1999 Microsoft Corporation. All rights reserved.

[26] see the book *Comparative Mythology* by Muata Ashby

[27] That there is an ultimate reality which is the substratum of all existence and which is common to all human beings is what is being referred to here.

[28] See the book *Initiation Into Egyptian Yoga* by Muata Ashby

[29] See the books *Egyptian Yoga Vol. 1* for more on the disciplines of Egyptian Yoga and *Mysteries of Isis* for more on the teachings of the Temple of Aset, by Muata Ashby

[30] ethics. (n.d.). *Dictionary.com Unabridged (v 1.1)*. Retrieved September 04, 2008, from Dictionary.com website: http://dictionary.reference.com/browse/ethics

[31] morals. (n.d.). *Dictionary.com Unabridged (v 1.1)*. Retrieved September 04, 2008, from Dictionary.com website: http://dictionary.reference.com/browse/morals

[32] the human being from Bende who himself is from God—Baluba of Kasayi in Congo-Kinshasa proverb

[33] *He who does not cultivate his field, will die of hunger.* -Ethiopia proverb

[34] The Blackwell Companion to Religious Ethics By William Schweiker, pp431

[35] *There is no phrase without a double meaning.* - Kenya proverb

[36] *A person should not over-indulge in silly habits.* -Tonga proverb

[37] *A proverb is the horse which can carry one swiftly to the discovery of ideas.* – Yoruba proverb

[38] *Keep your feet wherever you travel.* [*Expl:* People should maintain good morals wherever they might be.]-Tonga proverb

[39] Nkonsonkonso (link or chain). We are linked in both life and death. Those who share common blood relations never break apart. Symbol of human relations.

[41] *Introduction to African Religion Second Edition* by John S. Mbiti, *Morals in African Religion,*

[42] THE INSTRUCTION OF AMENEMOPE –Ancient Egyptian Wisdom Texts

[43] THE INSTRUCTION OF AMENEMOPE–Ancient Egyptian Wisdom Texts

[44] THE INSTRUCTION OF AMENEMOPE–Ancient Egyptian Wisdom Texts

[45] THE INSTRUCTIONS TO MERIKARE–Ancient Egyptian Wisdom Texts

[46] ibid

[47] *Every human being comes from God* –Baluba of Kasayi in Congo-Kinshasa proverb
*Cross the river in a crowd and the crocodile won't eat you.* -Ethiopia proverb
*If relatives help each other, what evil can hurt them?* -Ethiopia proverb
*When spider webs unite, they can tie up a lion.* -Ethiopia proverb

[50] Craig, Edward (1998). *Routledge Encyclopedia of Philosophy: Sociology of knowledge to Zaroastrianism.* Routledge (Taylor & Francis). ISBN 041516916X.

[51] Ghista, Dhanjoo N. (2004). *Socio-economic Democracy and the World Government.* World Scientific, p38. ISBN 9812385096.

[52] *"There are two roads traveled by humankind, those who seek to live MAAT and those who seek to satisfy their animal passions."* –Ancient Egyptian Proverb

[53] *"To suffer, is a necessity entailed upon your nature, would you prefer that miracles should protect you from its lessons or shalt you repine, because it happened unto you, when lo it happened unto all? Suffering is the golden cross upon which the rose of the Soul unfolds."* –Ancient Egyptian Proverb,

*Smooth seas do not make skillful sailors.* -African Proverb
[55] *As the wound inflames the finger, so thought inflames the mind.* - Galla proverb
[56] *Knowledge is like a garden: if it is not cultivated, it cannot be harvested.* - Cameroon
[57] *"The abomination of the sanctuary of GOD is: too much talking. Pray thou with a loving heart the petitions of which all are in secret. GOD will do thy business, hear that which thou say and will accept thine offerings."* –Ancient Egyptian Proverb
*He who talks incessantly talks nonsense.* - Ivory Coast
[58] Clothes put on while running come off while running. - Ethiopia proverb
[59] *"The Soul that hath no knowledge of the things that are or knowledge of their nature, is blinded by the body's passions and tossed about. The wretched Soul, not knowing what it is, becomes the slave of bodies of strange form in sorry plight, bearing the body as a load; not as the ruler but as the ruled."* –Ancient Egyptian Proverb
[60] *He who is free of faults, will never die.* -Buganda    Uganda proverb
*"Those who live today will die tomorrow, those who die tomorrow will be born again; Those who live MAAT will not die."* –Ancient Egyptian Proverb
[62] *"If a Soul on entering in the human body persists in its vice, it neither tastes deathlessness nor share in the Good; but speeding back again it turns into the path that leads to creeping things. This is the sentence of the vicious soul."* – Ancient Egyptian Proverb
[63] Two *buttocks do not fail to make a friction* – Tonga proverb
[64] *"If you meet a disputant who is not your equal or match, do not attack, they are weak. They will confound themselves. Do not answer the evil speech and give in to your animal passion for combat by venting your self against them. You will beat them through the reproof of the witnesses who will agree with you."* –Ancient Egyptian Proverb
[65] *Familiarity breeds contempt; distance breeds respect.* - Nigeria proverb
[66] *It takes two to make a quarrel.*-Ashanti    Ghana proverb
[67] *"Punish firmly and chastise soundly, then repression of crime becomes an example. But punishment except for crime will turn the complainer into an enemy."* –Ancient Egyptian Proverb
[68] *"Good things cease to be good in our wrong enjoyment of them. What nature meant to be pure sweetness, are then sources of bitterness to us; from such delights arise pain, from such joys, sorrows."* –Ancient Egyptian Proverb
[69] *Evil enters like a needle and spreads like an oak tree.* -Ashanti    Ghana proverb
[70] *A little subtleness is better than a lot of force.* - Zaire – The Congo proverb
[71] *" If your child accepts your words then no plan of theirs will go wrong. So teach your son to be a hearer, one who will be valued by the officials, one who will guide their speech by what they have been told, one who is regarded as a hearer. The children will reach old age if they listen to the wise words of their parents."* –Ancient Egyptian Proverb
*"If you are wise, train children to be pleasing to God. If they are straight and take after you, take good care of them. Do everything that is good for them. They are your children, your KA begot them. Don't withdraw your heart from them. But an offspring can make trouble. If they stray and neglect your council*

and disobey all that is said, with mouth spouting evil speech, then punish them for all their talk. –Ancient Egyptian Proverb

[72] see the book *Comparative Mythology* by Muata Ashby

[73] *"If you don't stand for something, you will fall for something."* - African Proverb

[74] *Mutual affection gives each his share.* -Galla Ethiopia proverb

[75] Self-actualisation is a term that has been used in various psychology theories, often in slightly different ways (e.g., Goldstein, Maslow, Rogers). The term was originally introduced by the organismic theorist Kurt Goldstein for the motive to realise all of one's potentialities. In his view, it is the master motive—indeed, the only real motive a person has, all others being merely manifestations of it. However, the concept was brought to prominence in Abraham Maslow's hierarchy of needs theory as the final level of psychological development that can be achieved when all basic and mental needs are fulfilled and the "actualisation" of the full personal potential takes place. According to Kurt Goldstein's book *The Organism: A Holistic Approach to Biology Derived from Pathological Data in Man*, self-actualization is "the tendency to actualize, as much as possible, [the organism's] individual capacities" in the world. The tendency to self-actualization is "the only drive by which the life of an organism is determined." (Goldstein 1995) Goldstein defined self-actualization as a driving life force that will ultimately lead to maximizing one's abilities and determine the path of one's life.

[76] *"Men and women are to become God-like through a life of virtue and the cultivation of the spirit through scientific knowledge, practice and bodily discipline."* –Ancient Egyptian Proverb

[77] *The African race is like an Indian rubber ball, the harder you dash it to the ground the higher it will rise.* – Bantu (African Proverbs by Gerd de Ley)

[78] see the books: *The Egyptian Book of the Dead* and *The 42 Precepts of Maat* by Muata Ashby

[79] Penpamsie (that which will not crush). "Penpamsie see bebirebe ahooden ne koroye." Unity in strength. [Ashanti mythology and adinkra symbols]

[80] *A cutting word is worse than a bowstring; a cut may heal, but the cut of the tongue does not.* - Mauritania proverb

[81] *(41) Do not speak falsely to a man, The God, abhors it; Do not sever your heart from your tongue, That all your strivings may succeed. You will be weighty before the others, And secure in the hand of The God. God hates the falsifier of words, He greatly abhors the dissembler...* THE INSTRUCTION OF AMENEMOPE –Ancient Egyptian Wisdom Texts

[82] *Where trust breaks down, peace breaks down.* -African Proverb

[83] *Truth keeps the hand cleaner than soap.* –Nigerian proverb

[85] *One falsehood spoils a thousand truths.* -Kenya proverb

[86] *Great events may stem from words of no importance.* -Kenya proverb

[87] *"Don't repeat slander nor should you even listen to it. It is the spouting of the hot bellied. Just report a thing that has been observed, not something that has been heard secondhand. If it is something negligible, don't even say anything. He who is standing before you will recognize your worth."* –Ancient Egyptian Proverb

[88] *The end of a lie is grief.* -Nigeria proverb

[89] *A cutting word is worse than a bowstring; a cut may heal, but the cut of the tongue does not* -Mauritania proverb

[90] *Happiness is openness to all people.* –African proverb

[91] *When the heart overflows, it comes out through the mouth.* – Ethiopia, *The heart of the wise man lies quiet like limpid water.* - Buganda proverb

[92] *He who does not know is forgiven by God* –Swahili proverb

[93] *A wise man who knows proverbs can reconcile difficulties.* -Niger proverb

[94] *The ruin of a nation begins in the homes of its people.* -Nigeria proverb/ Ashanti of Ghana proverb

[95] *"Punish firmly and chastise soundly, then repression of crime becomes an example. But punishment except for crime will turn the complainer into an enemy."* –Ancient Egyptian Proverb

[96] *The one who has wealth at home will not be partial,*
*He is a just man who lacks nothing. The poor man does not speak justly, Not righteous is one who says, "I wish I had...-* Ancient Egyptian proverb

[98] *When free men are given land, They work for you like a single team; No rebel will arise among them...-*Ancient Egyptian proverb

[100] Mframa-dan (wind house). House built to stand windy and treacherous conditions. [Ashanti mythology and adinkra symbols]

101 Dictionary.com Copyright © 2006, Lexico Publishing Group, LLC.

102 The American Humanist Association (AHA) is an American humanist group serving secular humanism, but tending to favor Humanism as defined by the world body for Humanism, the IHEU.

103 ibid

[104] *A people without a leader ruin the town.* –Ghananian proverb
*When emotions are societies objective, tyranny will govern regardless of the ruling class.* -Ancient Egyptian proverb

[105] Mmra krado (seal of the law). Symbolizing supreme authority. [Ashanti mythology and adinkra symbols]

[106] Kuntinkantan (do not boast). There is need for humility and servitude. [Ashanti mythology and adinkra symbols]

[107] *He whose refuses to obey cannot command.* -Kenyan proverb

[108] *The heart of the wise man lies quiet like limpid water.* -Cameroon proverb

[109] *A chief is like a rubbish heap; everything comes to him.* - African Proverb
*A leader is a donkey for others to ride.* - African Proverb

[110] *The strong do not need clubs.* –Senegalese proverb

[111] *A clear thinking leader is a sign of stability and an agent for change in society.* –Sierra Leonean proverb

[112] *To manage yourself, use your head to manage others, use your heart.* - African Proverb

[113] *A person who carries responsibility also receives blame.* -Kenyan proverb

[114] Ntesie-matemasie (I have heard and kept it). "Nyansa bun mu nne mate masie." Symbol of wisdom and knowledge. [Ashanti mythology and adinkra symbols]

[115] *When a king has good counselors, his reign is peaceful.* - Ashanti, Ghana proverb
(28) The Lord of the Two Shores is one who knows,
A king who has courtiers is not ignorant... -Instructions to Meri-Ka-Ra [Ancient Egyptian Wisdom Texts]

[116] *If you don't stand for something, you will fall for something.* - African Proverb

[117] *Leadership does not depend on age.* –Namibian proverb

[118] *A wise man who knows proverbs can reconcile difficulties.* - Niger proverb

[119] Threats and insults never rule a country –Zambian Proverb

[120] Two noisy waterfalls do not agree. –Kenyan proverb

[121] *If you are filled with pride, then you will have no room for wisdom.* – Tanzanian proverb

[122] *Arrogance burned the chief's compound.* –Ugandan proverb

[123] *When the moon is not full, the stars shine more brightly.* –Ugandan proverb

[124] WO NSA DA MU A "If your hands are in the dish" symbol of participatory government, democracy and pluralism From the aphorism, "Wo nsa da mu a, wonni nnya wo" -- "If your hands are in the dish, people do not eat everything and leave you nothing." Source: "Cloth As Metaphor" by G.F. Kojo Arthur

[125] WOFORO DUA PA A "when you climb a good tree" symbol of support, cooperation and encouragement From the expression "Woforo dua pa a, na yepia wo" meaning "When you climb a good tree, you are given a push". More metaphorically, it means that when you work for a good cause, you will get support.
Source: Cloth As Metaphor by G.F. Kojo Arthur

[126] *The leader who leads by pointing the way leaves no footprints for his followers.* - African Proverb

[127] *A wise man cannot save a decaying country as manure cannot save an eroding land.* - Ethiopian Proverb
*In the moment of crisis, the wise build bridges and foolish build dams.* - Nigerian proverb

[128] *Those exercising good habits and truth are leaders.* –Kenyan proverb

[129] Kontire ne Akwam (elders of the state). "Tikorommpam." One head does not constitute a council. [Ashanti mythology and adinkra symbols]

[130] *The man who has bread to eat does not appreciate the severity of a famine.* –Yoruba proverb
*The king who shuts his eyes during famine in the land will soon see ancestors.* -Nigerian proverb

[131] *He who dictates separates himself from others.* –Somali proverb

[132] *One person alone cannot rule the country* –Ethiopian Proverb
*One head alone does not go into council* -Ghanaian proverb
*One head does not contain all the wisdom* -Ghanaian proverb
*The elders of the village are the boundaries* -Ghanaian proverb

[133] *Consensus does not lead to easy decision making.* -Kenyan proverb

[134] *The owl merely sitting on a tree stump is not exercising chieftainship.* – Malawian proverb

[135] *If two wise men always agree, then there is no need for one of them.* – Zambian proverb
When the leaders are wise, so are the people. - Madagascar Proverbs

[136] *That which has been mutually agreed upon does not bring about disputes.* – Kenyan proverb

[137] see the book *The Collapse of Civilization and the Death of American Empire* by Muata Ashby

[138] John Stuart Mill. On Liberty, The Library of Liberal Arts edition, p.7. http://www.serendipity.li/jsmill/jsmill.htm

[139] *Federalist 10*, The **Federalist Papers** are a series of 85 articles advocating the ratification of the United States Constitution. Seventy-seven of the essays were published serially in *The Independent Journal* and *The New York Packet* between October 1787 and August 1788. A compilation of these and eight others, called ***The Federalist***, was published in 1788 by J. and A. McLean.

Jackson, Kenneth T. *The Encyclopedia of New York City*: The New York Historical Society; Yale University Press; 1995. p. 194.

[140] See Maurice Cranston's introduction to the *Social Contract*, Penguin Classics, 1968, pp. 9-42.

[141] for Spinoza's *mens una*, see Jonathan Israel, *Radical Enlightenment* (Oxford University Press, 2002), p. 274.

[142] Entry, "Rousseau" in the *Routelege Encyclopedia of Philosophy*, Edward Craig, editor, Volume Eight, p. 371

[143] see the book *The Collapse of Civilization and the Death of American Empire* by Muata Ashby

[144] other examples of Consensus Government include: Legislative Assembly of the Northwest Territories, Legislative Assembly of Nunavut

[145] ANANSE NTONTAN "spider's web" symbol of wisdom, creativity and the complexities of life

[146] NYANSAPO "wisdom knot" symbol of wisdom, ingenuity, intelligence and patience An especially revered symbol of the Akan, this symbol conveys the idea that "a wise person has the capacity to choose the best meeans to attain a goal. Being wise implies broad knowledge, learning and experience, and the ability to apply such faculties to practical ends." (Willis, "The Adinkra Dictionary")

[147] ADINKRAHENE greatness, charisma, leadership [Ashanti mythology and adinkra symbols]

[148] **Absolute monarchy** is a monarchical form of government where the king or queen has absolute power over all aspects of his/her subjects' lives.

[149] *A large chair does not make a king.* – Sudanese proverb

[150] See the book *Egyptian Mysteries Vol. 3: The Priests and Priestesses of Ancient Egypt* by Muata Ashby

[151] *When a king has good counselors, his reign is peaceful.* -Ethiopian proverb

[152] *Consensus does not lead to easy decision making.* - Kenyan proverb

[153] *Hunger is felt by a slave and hunger is felt by a king.* -Kenya proverb

[154] *A canoe does not know who is king - when it turns over, everyone gets wet.* – Wolof proverb

[155] *Looking at a king's mouth one would never think he sucked his mother's breast.* – Wolof proverb

[156] *A canoe does not know who is king - when it turns over, everyone gets wet.* – Wolof proverb

[157] *Hunger is felt by a slave and hunger is felt by a king.* -Kenya proverb

[158] *To love the king is not bad, but a king who loves you is better.* - Wolof proverb

[159] *The fate that befalls the lowly will befall the leader.* -Ugandan proverb

[160] *Who ever suggested that rats should become chiefs?* - Ugandan proverb

[161] *Even the king needs to be taught.* - Somali proverb

[162] *Other people's wisdom prevents the king from being called a fool The king who shuts his eyes during famine in the land will soon see ancestors. The king who shuts his eyes during famine in the land will soon see ancestors. - Nigerian proverb

[163] *A king cannot reign without the support of the elders.* -Burundian proverb

[164] The *multitude is stronger than a king.* - North African proverb

[165] *When a king reigns, it is thanks to the people; when a river sings, it is thanks to the stones.* - Wolof proverb

[166] A child without a mother is like a fish in shallow water.
-Mynamar Proverb
Children are the reward of life –Congo Proverb
[167] *A community without elders does not prosper.* –Mozambican proverb
[168] *If you watch your pot, your food will not burn.* -Niger proverb
[169] *I have not been an eavesdropper or pried into matters to make mischief.* –
Ancient Egyptian proverb
[170] *The house-roof fights with the rain, but he who is sheltered ignores it.* –
Wolof proverb
[171] Ese ne keterEma (the teeth and tongue). "Wonnwo ba ne se." No child is
born with its teeth. We improve and advance. [Ashanti mythology and adinkra
symbols]
[172] *The ruin of a nation begins in the homes of its people.*
   -Nigerian proverb
[173] *A child who did not listen grew horns on his forehead.* [*Expl:* There is a
Tonga tale which says that a certain animal asked for horns to be on its
forehead. When a drought came, this animal found it difficult to compete for
water from a steep well. The tale teaches people to heed other people's advice.
*Meaning:* A person who does not follow other peoples' advice runs into
trouble. –Tonga proverb
[174] *It is the duty of children to wait on elders, and not the elders on children.* -
Ashanti    Ghana proverb
[175] *It's a bad child who does not take advice.* -Ivory Coast proverb
[176] *If the child refuses to obey the rules, take him/her to the elephant to be
punished.* [*Expl:* Without following rules it is difficult for a child to acquire
good moral standards or behave properly. The proverb is used metaphorically.
The elephant is the most fearful and powerful animal. ] –Tonga proverb
[177] *Love is like a baby: it needs to be treated tenderly.*
-Congolese proverb
[178] *A child without a mother is like a fish in shallow water.*
-Mynamar proverb
[179] *Love is like a baby: it needs to be treated tenderly.* -Ethiopia proverb
[180] A bathing place you like best brings a crocodile bite. [*Expl:* We should be
careful with our lives lest we are overtaken by events. *Meaning:* Danger may
exist where you least expect it.] –Tonga proverb
[181] *"Every parent teaches as they act. They will speak to the children so that
they will speak to their children. They will set an example and not give
offence."* –Ancient Egyptian Proverb,
*When you follow in the path of your father, you learn to walk like him.-*
Ashanti, Ghana proverb
[182] *It takes a village to raise a child.* -West African proverb (Yoruba)
A child who doesn't listen to its mother will be brought up by the street. –Sierra
Leon Proverb
[183] *Kneeling you eat with others, keep standing and you eat nothing.* [*Expl:*
According to traditional etiquette, young people kneel in order to show respect
to their elders. *Meaning:* You learn a lot of things from elders when you are
humble, but not when you are rude.] –Tonga proverb
[184] KINTINKANTAN "puffed up extravagance" symbol of arrogance
[185] The bird that knows is different from the bird that understands. *There is a
difference between knowledge and wisdom.*-Sierra Leon proverb

[186] MATE MASIE "What I hear, I keep" symbol of wisdom, knowledge and prudence The implied meaning of the phrase "mate masie" is "I understand". Understanding means wisdom and knowledge, but it also represents the prudence of taking into consideration what another person has said.

[187] *Even though your mother has gray hair, she is still your mother.* –Tonga proverb

"Offer water to thy father and thy mother, who rest in the desert-valley… Omit not to do this, that thy son may do the like for thee." –Sage Ani [Ancient Egyptian Wisdom Texts]

[188] *Words of old people become fulfilled after a long time.* –Tonga proverb

[189] *The death of an elderly man is like a burning library* -Ivorian proverb

*A wise man who knows proverbs, reconciles difficulties* Yoruba proverb

[190] *You do not teach the paths of the forest to an old gorilla.* -Congolese proverb

[191] *A man who pays respect to the great paves the way for his own greatness.* -African Proverb

[192] *The elders of the village are the boundaries.* –Ghananian proverb

[193] BOA ME NA ME MMOA WO "Help me and let me help you" symbol of cooperation and interdependence Source: "Cloth As Metaphor" by G.F. Kojo Arthur

[194] ESE NE TEKREMA "the teeth and the tongue" symbol of friendship and interdependence The teeth and the tongue play interdependent roles in the mouth. They may come into conflict, but they need to work together.

[195] NKONSONKONSON "chain link" symbol of unity and human relations A reminder to contribute to the community, that in unity lies strength

[196] *When the village chief himself goes around inviting people to a meeting, know there is something wrong with the system.* –Malawian proverb

[197] *Want to go fast travel alone, want to go far travel with others* -African Proverb

[198] *Even a good-for-nothing fellow can carry a pot of palm wine to the funeral.* -Ewe proverb

[199] *He who learns, teaches.* -Ethiopian proverb

[200] *A village without a leader is destroyed by a single enemy* -African Proverb

[201] *When your neighbour is wrong you point a finger, but when you are wrong you hide.* -Ekonda proverb

[202] *Equality is difficult but superiority is painful* -African Proverb

[203] *What you expect others to do for you, do for them also* – Tonga proverb

[204] Never befoul the water. Do not lay waste the ploughed lands. -Ancient Egyptian Proverbs

[205] *The family is like a forest, if you are outside it is dense, if you are inside you see that each tree has its own position.* -Akhan proverb

[206] *God made the sea, we make the ship; He made the wind, we make the sail; He made the calm, we make the oars.* – Swahili proverb

[207] *Bad leaders are elected by poor citizens who do not vote.* -Kenyan proverb

*Crookedness does not lead cattle.* -Kenyan proverb

[208] *Be a mountain or lean on one.* –Somali proverb

[209] *When the heart overflows, it comes out through the mouth.* -Ethiopian proverb

*If you are a judge, don't stop a person from telling you everything they want to tell you. A person in distress wants to pour out their heart even more than they*

*want their case to be won. If you stop the person who is pleading, that person will say "why does this judge reject my plea?" Of course, not all that one pleads can be granted, but a good hearing soothes the heart. The means for getting a true and clear explanation is to listen with kindness.* —Ancient Egyptian Proverb

[210] *Occasion:* The proverb is used to advise people who have quarreled to reconcile and continue to live together. The proverb has a court setting or is cited at a council of elders where various cases are brought to be judged. Young people are advised to forgive each other if they have disagreed on certain issues. *TONGA PROVERBS FROM MALAWI* Copyright © 2001 by David K. Mphande

[211] *A wise man who knows proverbs, reconciles difficulties* Yoruba proverb

[212] The words from elders are like old chili which does not turn sour. -Tonga proverb

[213] *A person who does not follow other peoples' advice runs into trouble.* - Tonga proverb

[214] FUNTUNFUNEFU- DENKYEMFUNEFU "Siamese crocodiles" symbol of democracy and unity The Siamese crocodiles share one stomach, yet they fight over food. This popular symbol is a remind that infighting and tribalism is harmful to all who engage in it.

[215] AKOMA NTOSO "linked hearts" symbol of understanding and agreement

[216] HYE ANHYE - UNBURNABLE Symbol of the IMPERISHABILITY OF THE SELF, PERMANENCY OF THE HUMAN SOUL and TOUGHNESS - This represents the idea that GOD, the SPIRIT, never dies, or GOD lives forever. The Akan belief is that the human soul, an image of God, the Spirit, lives in perpetuity. Thus, there is life after the death of the physical part of the human being. [Ashanti mythology and adinkra symbols]

[217] Nyame nwu na mawu. If Nyame (God) dies, then I may die. Perpetual existence. [Ashanti mythology and adinkra symbols]

[218] Biribi wo soro. "Nyame biribi wo soro na ma embeka mensa (God there is something in the heavens, let it reach me.)." A symbol of hope. [Ashanti mythology and adinkra symbols]

[219] KERAPA - SANCTITY - Symbol of SANCTITY OF SELF, SPIRITUAL STRENGTH, GOOD SPIRIT, GOOD LUCK, and GOOD FORTUNE - Literal translation: Sanctity is part particle of the good; it is like a cat, it abhors filth; and it clears filth like the vulture does; that is why it is used to drive away evil and diseases. This symbol was woven into the bedside mat on which the king would step three times for good luck before going to bed. Every year, a cleaning ritual (*mmusuyidee*) was performed in the past. During the ceremony all streets of the townships were swept clean each morning and evening to remove mystical danger and to prevent disease or death from entering the township. [Ashanti mythology and adinkra symbols]

[220] NYAME NTI "by God's grace" symbol of faith and trust in God similar to Gye Nyame According to The Adinkra Dictionary by W. Bruce Willis: "This stalk is depicted as the staff of life in many cultures. It symbolizes to the Akan that food is a basis of life and that they could not survive if not for the food that God has placed here on Earth for their nourishment. "

[221] Nsoroma (a child of the heavens). "Obu Nyankon soroma te Nyame na onte neho so (A child of the Supreme Being I do not depend on myself. My

illumination is only a reflection of His.)." [Ashanti mythology and adinkra symbols]

222 GYE NYAME - EXCEPT GOD Symbol of the OMNIPOTENCE and the OMNIPRESENCE OF GOD [Ashanti mythology and adinkra symbols]

223 *"The Eye of Heru"* – The quintessential symbol of Ancient Egyptian religion and the human achievement of inner spiritual vision and higher consciousness. –Ancient Egypt

224 *The wise aim at boundaries beyond the present; they transcend the parameters of their origins.* –African Proverb

225 *If you want to send a message to God, tell it to the wind* -Ga proverb

226 *God conceals himself from the mind of man, but reveals himself to his heart.* –African Proverb

227 *To deny God's existence is like jumping with your eyes closed.* –Malagasy proverb

228 *Horns which are put on do not stick properly.* - South African proverb

229 *When one is in trouble one remembers God.* –Nigerian proverb

*To suffer, is a necessity entailed upon your nature, would you prefer that miracles should protect you from its lessons*

*or shalt you repine, because it happened unto you, when lo it happened unto all? Suffering is the golden cross upon*

*which the rose of the Soul unfolds.* –Ancient Egyptian proverb

230 Sankofa (return and fetch it). "SE wo werE fi na wosankofa a yenkyi." It is no taboo to return and fetch it when you forget. You can always undo your mistakes. [Ashanti mythology and adinkra symbols]

231 Hye wo nyhe (the one who burns you be not burned). Symbol of forgiveness. Turn the other cheek. [Ashanti mythology and adinkra symbols]

232 MPATAPO "knot of pacification/reconciliation" symbol of reconciliation, peacemaking and pacification Mpatapo represents the bond or knot that binds parties in a dispute to a peaceful, harmonious reconciliation. It is a symbol of peacemaking after strife.

233 *Do not kill, it does not serve you. Punish with beatings, with detention, Thus will the land be well ordered...* –Ancient Egyptian Proverb

234 *A cautious deer grows longer horns.* [*Expl:* If a deer wants to live long enough to grow impressive horns, it must be very careful with its life. The Tonga traditional way to kill game was to dig game-pits and cover them with branches. If an animal does not avoid the hedge then it will fall into the pit. The safest way is to avoid it.

*Meaning:* If one wants to live long one must be careful. Thus, people who are cautious usually avoid unnecessary danger.] –Tonga proverb

*If your child accepts your words then no plan of theirs will go wrong. So teach your son to be a hearer, one who will be valued by the officials, one who will guide their speech by what they have been told, one who is regarded as a hearer. The children will reach old age if they listen to the wise words of their parents.* –Ancient Egyptian Proverb

235 *The law is a spider's web; only the little insects get caught in it.* -Gambian proverb

236 AKOBEN "war horn" symbol of vigilance and wariness Akoben is a horn used to sound

237 *He who forgives ends the argument* -African Proverb

212

[238] *A silly daughter teaches her mother how to bear children.*
-Ethiopian proverb
[239] *Too large a morsel chokes the child.* – Mauritanian proverb
[240] *Advise and counsel him; if he does not listen, let adversity teach him.* -
Ethiopia proverb
[241] *Anger killed a mother cow.* - Ugandan proverb
*I have not allowed myself to become angry without cause.*
–Ancient Egyptian proverb
[242] *Knowledge is like a garden: if it is not cultivated, it cannot be harvested.* -
Cameroon proverb
"Eat not bread if another is suffering want, and thou dost not stretch out the
hand to him with bread….One is rich and another is poor. He that was rich in
past years is this year a groom. Be not greedy about filling the belly. The
course of the water of last year, it is this year in another place. "
-Sage Ani [Ancient Egyptian Wisdom Texts]
[243] *A man with too much ambition cannot sleep in peace.* - Baguirmi proverb
[244] *He who learns, teaches.* -Ethiopia proverb
[245] *"When opulence and extravagance are a necessity instead of righteousness
and truth, society will be governed by greed and injustice."* –Ancient Egyptian
Proverb
*"Ambition is to spiritual development what termites are to wood."* –Ancient
Egyptian Proverb
[246] *Then they all fall over onto their backs assenting by clapping their hands
and saying, "Be appeased, be appeased."*
*Expl:* This is a proverbial prayer in Tonga traditional religion. It is a request
that the spirit should go away to the spirit-land and leave the living or, if it
continues to interfere in their affairs, that the spirit might work only for the
good of its friends/relations, and provide them with abundance of the desirable
things of life.
*Occasion:* The proverb is used at a traditional worship, when offering sacrifices
to the ancestors as one way of appeasing them or seeking their favour. –Tonga
proverb
The Ancient Egyptian symbol □□(*HETEP* - Supreme Peace) is one of the
primary ritual objects and acts that is performed to promote appeasement
[peace] between humans and spirit.
[247] Discipline given at the Temple of Aset {Isis} in Kamit (Ancient Egypt) see
the books, *The Mysteries of Isis* by Muata Ashby and *Initiation into Egyptian
Yoga and Neterian Spirituality* by Muata Ashby
[248] Hieroglyphic translation presented by Dr. Muata Ashby at the 2007 Neterian
Conference, based on the Teaching of the Temple of Aset, myth of Ra and
Aset.
[249] In Chapter 125 of the Book of the Dead, the person uttering the declarations
states:
*"I have done God's will. I have given bread to the hungry, water to the thirsty,
clothes to the clotheless and a boat to those who were shipwrecked. I made the
prescribed offerings to the gods and goddesses and I also made offerings in the
temple to the glorious spirits. Therefore, protect me when I go to face The
God."*
[250] *"Do good because of tomorrow"* -Ghanaian Waalli proverb

[251] *If your house is burning, there is not time to go hunting.* - West Africa proverb

[252] *If you don't stand for something, you will fall for something.* - Africa proverb

[253] The American Heritage® Dictionary of the English Language, Fourth Edition Copyright © 2000 by Houghton Mifflin Company.

[254] *Based on the Random House Dictionary, © Random House, Inc. 2009.*

[255] The American Heritage® Dictionary of the English Language, Fourth Edition Copyright © 2000 by Houghton Mifflin Company.

[256] *ibid*

[257] *Kill Them All and Let God Sort Them Out* The quote above is attributed to Arnaud-Armaury, the Abbot of Citeaux, and "spiritual advisor" to the Albigensian Crusade. Pope Innocent III ordered the Albigensian Crusade, to purge southern France of the Cathari heretics. It began in the summer of 1209, with their first target - the town of Beziers. The Catholic faithful in Beziers refused to give up the Catharis among themselves. The crusaders invaded. When Arnaud-Amaury was asked whom to kill he replied "Kill them all. God will know his own." They did. The crusaders slaughtered nearly everyone in town, over 20,000, either burned or clubbed to death. Thus they achieved their goal of killing the estimated 200 heretics who were hiding in the town among the Catholic faithful.
http://www.manbottle.com/triva/Kill_them_all....htm_answzer.htm

[258] someone who sees the world in terms of ideological concepts to be upheld regardless of their rightness or wrongness because of their moralistic outlook, the world is black or white, "I am right and others are wrong" and there is no compromise, no capacity to allow others to be wrong in the moralist's eyes.

[259] *ibid*

[260] See *The Collapse of Civilization and Death of American Empire* by Muata Ashby

[261] See the books: *The Collapse of Civilization and Death of American Empire* and *Dollar Crisis* by Muata Ashby

[262] "It's all going to end very badly": A capitalist worries
Alan Greenspan's Feb. 26 testimony before the Senate Banking Committee was deadly dull. The workers, of course, were not expected to pay attention. But he made telling remarks about the low-wage trend that he's afraid is in danger-and the "preemptive" strike he's preparing. Greenspan said: "Atypical restraint on compensation increases has been evident for a few years now and appears to be mainly the consequence of greater worker insecurity. ... The reluctance of workers to leave their jobs to seek other employment as the labor market tightened has provided further evidence of such concern, as has the tendency toward longer labor union contracts. ..."The low level of work stoppages of recent years also attests to concern about job security. Thus the willingness of workers in recent years to trade off smaller increases in wages for greater job security seems to be reasonably well documented. ...
http://www.workers.org/ww/1997/greenspan2.html

[263] The double plumes of the two Maat Goddesses of Ancient Egypt; they represent the double truth, that of the physical world and that of the Spirit that is to be attained by a righteous person who wants to attain the highest goal of life, spiritual emancipation.

[264] Random House Encyclopedia Copyright (C) 1983,1990 by Random House Inc.

[265] Humanism. (n.d.). *Dictionary.com Unabridged (v 1.1)*. Retrieved September 06, 2008, from Dictionary.com website:
http://dictionary.reference.com/browse/Humanism

[266] ibid

[267] see the book *Introduction to Maat Philosophy* by Muata Ashby

[268] For the full text see the *Book of the Dead* by Muata Ashby

269 Guns, Germs, and Steel by Jared Diamond

270 1. a delusional mental disorder that is marked by infantile feelings of personal omnipotence and grandeur Source: *Merriam-Webster's Medical Dictionary, © 2002 Merriam-Webster, Inc.* 2. A psychopathological condition characterized by delusional fantasies of wealth, power, or omnipotence. *The American Heritage® Dictionary of the English Language, Fourth Edition Copyright © 2000 by Houghton Mifflin Company.*

[271] See *The Collapse of Civilization and Death of American Empire* by Muata Ashby

[272] See *The Collapse of Civilization and Death of American Empire* by Muata Ashby

# REFERENCES TO AFRICAN PROVERBS

*African Origins of Civilization* by Muata Ashby
*African Proverbs* by Gerd de Ley
*Comparative Mythology* by Muata Ashby
*Egyptian Proverbs* by Muata Ashby
*Egyptian Yoga Vol. 1* by Muata Ashby
http://africanhistory.about.com/library/weekly/aaAdinkra.ht
    m
http://africawithin.com/tour/ghana/adinkra_symbols.htm
http://cogweb.ucla.edu/Discourse/Proverbs/Ashanti.html
http://www.famous-proverbs.com/african.htm
http://www.marshall.edu/akanart/akancosmology.html
http://www.princetonol.com/groups/iad/lessons/middle/af-
    prov2.htm
*Initiation Into Egyptian Yoga* by Muata Ashby
*Introduction to African Religion Second Edition* by John S.
    Mbiti, *Morals in African Religion,*
*Introduction to Maat Philosophy* by Muata Ashby
*Mysteries of Isis* by Muata Ashby
*Proverbs for Preaching and Teaching series* -Series Editor,
    Joshua N. Kudadjie
*The 42 Precepts of Maat* by Muata Ashby
*The Black Ancient Egyptians* by Muata Ashby
*The Collapse of Civilization and Death of American
    Empire* by Muata Ashby
*The Egyptian Book of the Dead* by Muata Ashby

# INDEX

## OTHER BOOKS BY THE AUTHOR

# SEMA INSTITUTE

Cruzian Mystic P.O. Box 570459, Miami, Florida. 33257
(305) 378-6253, Fax. (305) 378-6253

## Other Books From C M Books

P.O.Box 570459
Miami, Florida, 33257
(305) 378-6253 Fax: (305) 378-6253

This book is part of a series on the study and practice of Ancient Egyptian Yoga and Mystical Spirituality based on the writings of Dr. Muata Abhaya Ashby. They are also part of the Egyptian Yoga Course provided by the Sema Institute of Yoga. Below you will find a listing of the other books in this series. For more information send for the Egyptian Yoga Book-Audio-Video Catalog or the Egyptian Yoga Course Catalog.

Now you can study the teachings of Egyptian and Indian Yoga wisdom and Spirituality with the Egyptian Yoga Mystical Spirituality Series. The Egyptian Yoga Series takes you through the Initiation process and lead you to understand the mysteries of the soul and the Divine and to attain the highest goal of life: ENLIGHTENMENT. The *Egyptian Yoga Series*, takes you on an in depth study of Ancient Egyptian mythology and their inner mystical meaning. Each Book is prepared for the serious student of the mystical sciences and provides a study of the teachings along with exercises, assignments and projects to make the teachings understood and effective in real life. The Series is part of the Egyptian Yoga course but may be purchased even if you are not taking the course. The series is ideal for study groups.

**Prices subject to change.**

1. *EGYPTIAN YOGA: THE PHILOSOPHY OF ENLIGHTENMENT* An original, fully illustrated work,

including hieroglyphs, detailing the meaning of the Egyptian mysteries, tantric yoga, psycho-spiritual and physical exercises. Egyptian Yoga is a guide to the practice of the highest spiritual philosophy which leads to absolute freedom from human misery and to immortality. It is well known by scholars that Egyptian philosophy is the basis of Western and Middle Eastern religious philosophies such as *Christianity, Islam, Judaism,* the *Kabala,* and Greek philosophy, but what about Indian philosophy, Yoga and Taoism? What were the original teachings? How can they be practiced today? What is the source of pain and suffering in the world and what is the solution? Discover the deepest mysteries of the mind and universe within and outside of your self. 8.5" X 11" ISBN: 1-884564-01-1 Soft $19.95

2.      *EGYPTIAN YOGA: African Religion Volume 2-* Theban Theology U.S. In this long awaited sequel to *Egyptian Yoga: The Philosophy of Enlightenment* you will take a fascinating and enlightening journey back in time and discover the teachings which constituted the epitome of Ancient Egyptian spiritual wisdom. What are the disciplines which lead to the fulfillment of all desires? Delve into the three states of consciousness (waking, dream and deep sleep) and the fourth state which transcends them all, Neberdjer, "The Absolute." These teachings of the city of Waste (Thebes) were the crowning achievement of the Sages of Ancient Egypt. They establish the standard mystical keys for understanding the profound mystical symbolism of the Triad of human consciousness. ISBN 1-884564-39-9 $23.95

3.      *THE KEMETIC DIET: GUIDE TO HEALTH, DIET AND FASTING* Health issues have always been important to human beings since the beginning of time. The earliest records of history show that the art of healing was held in high esteem since the time of Ancient Egypt. In the early 20th century, medical doctors had almost attained the status of sainthood by the promotion of the idea that they alone were "scientists" while other healing modalities and traditional healers who did not follow the "scientific method' were nothing but superstitious, ignorant charlatans who at best would take the money of their clients and at worst kill them with the unscientific "snake oils" and "irrational theories". In the late 20th century, the failure of the modern medical establishment's

ability to lead the general public to good health, promoted the move by many in society towards "alternative medicine". Alternative medicine disciplines are those healing modalities which do not adhere to the philosophy of allopathic medicine. Allopathic medicine is what medical doctors practice by an large. It is the theory that disease is caused by agencies outside the body such as bacteria, viruses or physical means which affect the body. These can therefore be treated by medicines and therapies   The natural healing method began in the absence of extensive technologies with the idea that all the answers for health may be found in nature or rather, the deviation from nature. Therefore, the health of the body can be restored by correcting the aberration and thereby restoring balance. This is the area that will be covered in this volume. Allopathic techniques have their place in the art of healing. However, we should not forget that the body is a grand achievement of the spirit and built into it is the capacity to maintain itself and heal itself. Ashby, Muata ISBN: 1-884564-49-6          $28.95

4.       INITIATION INTO EGYPTIAN YOGA Shady: Spiritual discipline or program, to go deeply into the mysteries, to study the mystery teachings and literature profoundly, to penetrate the mysteries. You will learn about the mysteries of initiation into the teachings and practice of Yoga and how to become an Initiate of the mystical sciences. This insightful manual is the first in a series which introduces you to the goals of daily spiritual and yoga practices: Meditation, Diet, Words of Power and the ancient wisdom teachings.   8.5" X 11" ISBN 1-884564-02-X   Soft Cover $24.95 U.S.

5.       *THE AFRICAN ORIGINS OF CIVILIZATION, RELIGION AND YOGA SPIRITUALITY AND ETHICS PHILOSOPHY* HARD COVER EDITION Part 1, Part 2, Part 3 in one volume 683 Pages Hard Cover First Edition Three volumes in one. Over the past several years I have been asked to put together in one volume the most important evidences showing the correlations and common teachings between Kamiah (Ancient Egyptian) culture and religion and that of India. The questions of the history of Ancient Egypt, and the latest archeological evidences showing civilization and culture in Ancient Egypt and its spread to other countries, has intrigued many scholars as well as mystics over the years. Also, the possibility that

Ancient Egyptian Priests and Priestesses migrated to Greece, India and other countries to carry on the traditions of the Ancient Egyptian Mysteries, has been speculated over the years as well. In chapter 1 of the book *Egyptian Yoga The Philosophy of Enlightenment,* 1995, I first introduced the deepest comparison between Ancient Egypt and India that had been brought forth up to that time. Now, in the year 2001 this new book, *THE AFRICAN ORIGINS OF CIVILIZATION, MYSTICAL RELIGION AND YOGA PHILOSOPHY,* more fully explores the motifs, symbols and philosophical correlations between Ancient Egyptian and Indian mysticism and clearly shows not only that Ancient Egypt and India were connected culturally but also spiritually. How does this knowledge help the spiritual aspirant? This discovery has great importance for the Yogis and mystics who follow the philosophy of Ancient Egypt and the mysticism of India. It means that India has a longer history and heritage than was previously understood. It shows that the mysteries of Ancient Egypt were essentially a yoga tradition which did not die but rather developed into the modern day systems of Yoga technology of India. It further shows that African culture developed Yoga Mysticism earlier than any other civilization in history. All of this expands our understanding of the unity of culture and the deep legacy of Yoga, which stretches into the distant past, beyond the Indus Valley civilization, the earliest known high culture in India as well as the Vedic tradition of Aryan culture. Therefore, Yoga culture and mysticism is the oldest known tradition of spiritual development and Indian mysticism is an extension of the Ancient Egyptian mysticism. By understanding the legacy which Ancient Egypt gave to India the mysticism of India is better understood and by comprehending the heritage of Indian Yoga, which is rooted in Ancient Egypt the Mysticism of Ancient Egypt is also better understood. This expanded understanding allows us to prove the underlying kinship of humanity, through the common symbols, motifs and philosophies which are not disparate and confusing teachings but in reality expressions of the same study of truth through metaphysics and mystical realization of Self. (HARD COVER) ISBN: 1-884564-50-X   $45.00 U.S.   81/2" X 11"

6.      *AFRICAN ORIGINS BOOK 1 PART 1* African Origins of African Civilization, Religion, Yoga Mysticism and Ethics Philosophy-Soft Cover $24.95 ISBN: 1-884564-55-0

7.      *AFRICAN ORIGINS BOOK 2 PART 2* African Origins of Western Civilization, Religion and Philosophy (Soft) -Soft Cover $24.95 ISBN: 1-884564-56-9

8.      *EGYPT AND INDIA AFRICAN ORIGINS OF Eastern Civilization, Religion, Yoga Mysticism and Philosophy*-Soft Cover $29.95 (Soft) ISBN: 1-884564-57-7

9.      *THE MYSTERIES OF ISIS: **The Ancient Egyptian Philosophy of Self-Realization*** - There are several paths to discover the Divine and the mysteries of the higher Self. This volume details the mystery teachings of the goddess Aset (Isis) from Ancient Egypt- the path of wisdom. It includes the teachings of her temple and the disciplines that are enjoined for the initiates of the temple of Aset as they were given in ancient times. Also, this book includes the teachings of the main myths of Aset that lead a human being to spiritual enlightenment and immortality.  Through the study of ancient myth and the illumination of initiatic understanding the idea of God is expanded from the mythological comprehension to the metaphysical. Then this metaphysical understanding is related to you, the student, so as to begin understanding your true divine nature. ISBN 1-884564-24-0  $22.99

10.     *EGYPTIAN PROVERBS:* collection of —Ancient Egyptian Proverbs and Wisdom Teachings -How to live according to MAAT Philosophy. Beginning Meditation. All proverbs are indexed for easy searches. For the first time in one volume, — —Ancient Egyptian Proverbs, wisdom teachings and meditations, fully illustrated with hieroglyphic text and symbols. EGYPTIAN PROVERBS is a unique collection of knowledge and wisdom which you can put into practice today and transform your life. $14.95 U.S      ISBN: 1-884564-00-3

11.     *GOD OF LOVE: THE PATH OF DIVINE LOVE The Process of Mystical Transformation and The Path of Divine Love* This Volume focuses on the ancient wisdom teachings of "Neter Merri" –the Ancient Egyptian philosophy of Divine

231

Love and how to use them in a scientific process for self-transformation. Love is one of the most powerful human emotions. It is also the source of Divine feeling that unifies God and the individual human being. When love is fragmented and diminished by egoism the Divine connection is lost. The Ancient tradition of Neter Merri leads human beings back to their Divine connection, allowing them to discover their innate glorious self that is actually Divine and immortal. This volume will detail the process of transformation from ordinary consciousness to cosmic consciousness through the integrated practice of the teachings and the path of Devotional Love toward the Divine. 5.5"x 8.5" ISBN 1-884564-11-9 $22.95

12. *INTRODUCTION TO MAAT PHILOSOPHY: Spiritual Enlightenment Through the Path of Virtue* Known commonly as Karma in India, the teachings of MAAT contain an extensive philosophy based on ariu (deeds) and their fructification in the form of shai and renenet (fortune and destiny, leading to Meskhenet (fate in a future birth) for living virtuously and with orderly wisdom are explained and the student is to begin practicing the precepts of Maat in daily life so as to promote the process of purification of the heart in preparation for the judgment of the soul. This judgment will be understood not as an event that will occur at the time of death but as an event that occurs continuously, at every moment in the life of the individual. The student will learn how to become allied with the forces of the Higher Self and to thereby begin cleansing the mind (heart) of impurities so as to attain a higher vision of reality. ISBN 1-884564-20-8 $22.99

13. *MEDITATION The Ancient Egyptian Path to Enlightenment* Many people do not know about the rich history of meditation practice in Ancient Egypt. This volume outlines the theory of meditation and presents the Ancient Egyptian Hieroglyphic text which give instruction as to the nature of the mind and its three modes of expression. It also presents the texts which give instruction on the practice of meditation for spiritual Enlightenment and unity with the Divine. This volume allows the reader to begin practicing meditation by explaining, in easy to understand terms, the simplest form of meditation and working up to the most advanced form which was practiced in

ancient times and which is still practiced by yogis around the world in modern times. ISBN 1-884564-27-7  $22.99

14.   *THE GLORIOUS LIGHT MEDITATION* TECHNIQUE OF ANCIENT EGYPT New for the year 2000. This volume is based on the earliest known instruction in history given for the practice of formal meditation. Discovered by Dr. Muata Ashby, it is inscribed on the walls of the Tomb of Seti I in Thebes Egypt. This volume details the philosophy and practice of this unique system of meditation originated in Ancient Egypt and the earliest practice of meditation known in the world which occurred in the most advanced African Culture. ISBN: 1-884564-15-1 $16.95 (PB)

15.   *THE SERPENT POWER:   The Ancient Egyptian Mystical Wisdom of the Inner Life Force.*   This Volume specifically deals with the latent life Force energy of the universe and in the human body, its control and sublimation. How to develop the Life Force energy of the subtle body. This Volume will introduce the esoteric wisdom of the science of how virtuous living acts in a subtle and mysterious way to cleanse the latent psychic energy conduits and vortices of the spiritual body. ISBN 1-884564-19-4   $22.95

16.   *EGYPTIAN YOGA The Postures of The Gods and Goddesses* Discover the physical postures and exercises practiced thousands of years ago in Ancient Egypt which are today known as Yoga exercises. Discover the history of the postures and how they were transferred from Ancient Egypt in Africa to India through Buddhist Tantrism. Then practice the postures as you discover the mythic teaching that originally gave birth to the postures and was practiced by the Ancient Egyptian priests and priestesses. This work is based on the pictures and teachings from the Creation story of Ra, The Asarian Resurrection Myth and the carvings and reliefs from various Temples in Ancient Egypt 8.5" X 11" ISBN 1-884564-10-0 Soft Cover $21.95      Exercise video   $20

17.   *SACRED SEXUALITY: EGYPTIAN TANTRA YOGA: The Art of Sex* Sublimation and Universal Consciousness This Volume will expand on the male and female principles within the human body and in the universe and further detail the sublimation of sexual energy into spiritual energy. The student

will study the deities Min and Hathor, Asar and Aset, Geb and Nut and discover the mystical implications for a practical spiritual discipline. This Volume will also focus on the Tantric aspects of Ancient Egyptian and Indian mysticism, the purpose of sex and the mystical teachings of sexual sublimation which lead to self-knowledge and Enlightenment. 5.5"x 8.5"  ISBN 1-884564-03-8      $24.95

18.    *AFRICAN RELIGION Volume 4: ASARIAN THEOLOGY: RESURRECTING OSIRIS* The path of Mystical Awakening and the Keys to Immortality NEW REVISED AND EXPANDED EDITION!   The Ancient Sages created stories based on human and superhuman beings whose struggles, aspirations, needs and desires ultimately lead them to discover their true Self. The myth of Aset, Asar and Heru is no exception in this area. While there is no one source where the entire story may be found, pieces of it are inscribed in various ancient Temples walls, tombs, steles and papyri.  For the first time available, the complete myth of Asar, Aset and Heru has been compiled from original Ancient Egyptian, Greek and Coptic Texts. This epic myth has been richly illustrated with reliefs from the Temple of Heru at Edfu, the Temple of Aset at Philae, the Temple of Asar at Abydos, the Temple of Hathor at Denderah and various papyri, inscriptions and reliefs. Discover the myth which inspired the teachings of the *Shetaut Neter* (Egyptian Mystery System - Egyptian Yoga) and the Egyptian Book of Coming Forth By Day. Also, discover the three levels of Ancient Egyptian Religion, how to understand the mysteries of the Duat or Astral World and how to discover the abode of the Supreme in the Amenta, *The Other World* The ancient religion of Asar, Aset and Heru, if properly understood, contains all of the elements necessary to lead the sincere aspirant to attain immortality through inner self-discovery.  This volume presents the entire myth and explores the main mystical themes and rituals associated with the myth for understating human existence, creation and the way to achieve spiritual emancipation - *Resurrection.* The Asarian myth is so powerful that it influenced and is still having an effect on the major world religions. Discover the origins and mystical meaning of the Christian Trinity, the Eucharist ritual and the ancient origin of the birthday of Jesus Christ. Soft Cover ISBN: 1-884564-27-5 $24.95

19.     *THE EGYPTIAN BOOK OF THE DEAD MYSTICISM OF THE PERT EM HERU* " I Know myself, I know myself, I am One With God!–From the Pert Em Heru "The Ru Pert em Heru" or "Ancient Egyptian Book of The Dead," or "Book of Coming Forth By Day" as it is more popularly known, has fascinated the world since the successful translation of Ancient Egyptian hieroglyphic scripture over 150 years ago. The astonishing writings in it reveal that the Ancient Egyptians believed in life after death and in an ultimate destiny to discover the Divine. The elegance and aesthetic beauty of the hieroglyphic text itself has inspired many see it as an art form in and of itself. But is there more to it than that? Did the Ancient Egyptian wisdom contain more than just aphorisms and hopes of eternal life beyond death? In this volume Dr. Muata Ashby, the author of over 25 books on Ancient Egyptian Yoga Philosophy has produced a new translation of the original texts which uncovers a mystical teaching underlying the sayings and rituals instituted by the Ancient Egyptian Sages and Saints. "Once the philosophy of Ancient Egypt is understood as a mystical tradition instead of as a religion or primitive mythology, it reveals its secrets which if practiced today will lead anyone to discover the glory of spiritual self-discovery. The Pert em Heru is in every way comparable to the Indian Upanishads or the Tibetan Book of the Dead." □ $28.95      ISBN# 1-884564-28-3 Size: 8½" X 11

20.     *African Religion VOL. 1- ANUNIAN THEOLOGY THE MYSTERIES OF RA* The Philosophy of Anu and The Mystical Teachings of The Ancient Egyptian  Creation Myth Discover the mystical teachings contained in the Creation Myth and the gods and goddesses who brought creation and human beings into existence. The Creation myth of Anu is the source of Anunian Theology but also of the other main theological systems of Ancient Egypt that also influenced other world religions including Christianity, Hinduism and Buddhism. The Creation Myth holds the key to understanding the universe and for attaining spiritual Enlightenment. ISBN: 1-884564-38-0 $19.95

21.     *African Religion VOL  3: Memphite Theology: MYSTERIES OF MIND* Mystical Psychology & Mental Health for Enlightenment and Immortality based on the Ancient Egyptian

Philosophy of Menefer -Mysticism of Ptah, Egyptian Physics and Yoga Metaphysics and the Hidden properties of Matter. This volume uncovers the mystical psychology of the Ancient Egyptian wisdom teachings centering on the philosophy of the Ancient Egyptian city of Menefer (Memphite Theology). How to understand the mind and how to control the senses and lead the mind to health, clarity and mystical self-discovery. This Volume will also go deeper into the philosophy of God as creation and will explore the concepts of modern science and how they correlate with ancient teachings. This Volume will lay the ground work for the understanding of the philosophy of universal consciousness and the initiatic/yogic insight into who or what is God? ISBN 1-884564-07-0    $22.95

22.    *AFRICAN RELIGION VOLUME 5: THE GODDESS AND THE EGYPTIAN MYSTERIESTHE PATH OF THE GODDESS THE GODDESS PATH* The Secret Forms of the Goddess and the Rituals of Resurrection The Supreme Being may be worshipped as father or as mother. *Ushet Rekhat* or *Mother Worship*, is the spiritual process of worshipping the Divine in the form of the Divine Goddess. It celebrates the most important forms of the Goddess including *Nathor, Maat, Aset, Arat, Amentet and Hathor* and explores their mystical meaning as well as the rising of *Sirius,* the star of Aset (Aset) and the new birth of Hor (Heru). The end of the year is a time of reckoning, reflection and engendering a new or renewed positive movement toward attaining spiritual Enlightenment. The Mother Worship devotional meditation ritual, performed on five days during the month of December and on New Year's Eve, is based on the Ushet Rekhit. During the ceremony, the cosmic forces, symbolized by Sirius - and the constellation of Orion ---, are harnessed through the understanding and devotional attitude of the participant. This propitiation draws the light of wisdom and health to all those who share in the ritual, leading to prosperity and wisdom. $14.95 ISBN 1-884564-18-6

23.    *THE MYSTICAL JOURNEY FROM JESUS TO CHRIST* Discover the ancient Egyptian origins of Christianity before the Catholic Church and learn the mystical teachings given by Jesus to assist all humanity in becoming Christlike. Discover the secret meaning of the Gospels that were discovered in Egypt. Also discover how and why so many Christian

churches came into being. Discover that the Bible still holds the keys to mystical realization even though its original writings were changed by the church. Discover how to practice the original teachings of Christianity which leads to the Kingdom of Heaven. $24.95     ISBN# 1-884564-05-4 size: 8½" X 11"

24.    *THE STORY OF ASAR, ASET AND HERU:* An Ancient Egyptian Legend (For Children)     Now for the first time, the most ancient myth of Ancient Egypt comes alive for children. Inspired by the books *The Asarian Resurrection: The Ancient Egyptian Bible* and *The Mystical Teachings of The Asarian Resurrection, The Story of Asar, Aset and Heru* is an easy to understand and thrilling tale which inspired the children of Ancient Egypt to aspire to greatness and righteousness.     If you and your child have enjoyed stories like *The Lion King* and *Star Wars you will love The Story of Asar, Aset and Heru.* Also, if you know the story of Jesus and Krishna you will discover than Ancient Egypt had a similar myth and that this myth carries important spiritual teachings for living a fruitful and fulfilling life.  This book may be used along with *The Parents Guide To The Asarian Resurrection Myth: How to Teach Yourself and Your Child the Principles of Universal Mystical Religion.* The guide provides some background to the Asarian Resurrection myth and it also gives insight into the mystical teachings contained in it which you may introduce to your child. It is designed for parents who wish to grow spiritually with their children and it serves as an introduction for those who would like to study the Asarian Resurrection Myth in depth and to practice its teachings. 8.5" X 11" ISBN: 1-884564-31-3   $12.95

25.    *THE    PARENTS    GUIDE    TO    THE    AUSARIAN RESURRECTION MYTH:* How to Teach Yourself and Your Child  the Principles of Universal Mystical Religion.    This insightful manual brings for the timeless wisdom of the ancient through the Ancient Egyptian myth of Asar, Aset and Heru and the mystical teachings contained in it for parents who want to guide their children to understand and practice the teachings of mystical spirituality. This manual may be used with the children's storybook *The Story of Asar, Aset and Heru* by Dr. Muata Abhaya Ashby.     ISBN: 1-884564-30-5 $16.95

26.   *HEALING THE CRIMINAL HEART.* Introduction to Maat
Philosophy, Yoga and Spiritual Redemption Through the Path
of Virtue    Who is a criminal? Is there such a thing as a
criminal heart? What is the source of evil and sinfulness and is
there any way to rise above it? Is there redemption for those
who have committed sins, even the worst crimes?    Ancient
Egyptian mystical psychology holds important answers to
these questions. Over ten thousand years ago mystical
psychologists, the Sages of Ancient Egypt, studied and charted
the human mind and spirit and laid out a path which will lead
to spiritual redemption, prosperity and Enlightenment.    This
introductory volume brings forth the teachings of the Asarian
Resurrection, the most important myth of Ancient Egypt, with
relation to the faults of human existence: anger, hatred, greed,
lust, animosity, discontent, ignorance, egoism jealousy,
bitterness, and a myriad of psycho-spiritual ailments which
keep a human being in a state of negativity and adversity
ISBN: 1-884564-17-8    $15.95

27.   *TEMPLE   RITUAL   OF   THE   ANCIENT   EGYPTIAN
MYSTERIES--THEATER  &  DRAMA  OF  THE  ANCIENT
EGYPTIAN MYSTERIES*: Details the practice of the mysteries
and ritual program of the temple and the philosophy an
practice of the ritual of the mysteries, its purpose and
execution. Featuring the Ancient Egyptian stage play-"The
Enlightenment of Hathor' Based on an Ancient Egyptian
Drama, The original Theater -Mysticism of the Temple of
Hetheru 1-884564-14-3 $19.95   By Dr. Muata Ashby

28.       GUIDE TO PRINT ON DEMAND: SELF-PUBLISH FOR PROFIT,
SPIRITUAL  FULFILLMENT  AND  SERVICE  TO  HUMANITY
Everyone asks us how we produced so many books in such a
short time. Here are the secrets to writing and producing books
that uplift humanity and how to get them printed for a fraction
of the regular cost. Anyone can become an author even if they
have limited funds. All that is necessary is the willingness to
learn how the printing and book business work and the desire
to follow the special instructions given here for preparing your
manuscript format. Then you take your work directly to the
non-traditional companies who can produce your books for
less than the traditional book printer can. ISBN: 1-884564-40-
2    $16.95 U. S.

29.     *Egyptian Mysteries: Vol. 1,* Shetaut Neter What are the Mysteries? For thousands of years the spiritual tradition of Ancient Egypt, S*hetaut Neter,* "The Egyptian Mysteries," "The Secret Teachings," have fascinated, tantalized and amazed the world. At one time exalted and recognized as the highest culture of the world, by Africans, Europeans, Asiatics, Hindus, Buddhists and other cultures of the ancient world, in time it was shunned by the emerging orthodox world religions. Its temples desecrated, its philosophy maligned, its tradition spurned, its philosophy dormant in the mystical *Medu Neter*, the mysterious hieroglyphic texts which hold the secret symbolic meaning that has scarcely been discerned up to now. What are the secrets of *Nehast* {spiritual awakening and emancipation, resurrection}. More than just a literal translation, this volume is for awakening to the secret code *Shetitu* of the teaching which was not deciphered by Egyptologists, nor could be understood by ordinary spiritualists. This book is a reinstatement of the original science made available for our times, to the reincarnated followers of Ancient Egyptian culture and the prospect of spiritual freedom to break the bonds of *Khemn,* "ignorance," and slavery to evil forces: *Såaa* . ISBN: 1-884564-41-0 $19.99

30.     *EGYPTIAN MYSTERIES VOL 2:* Dictionary of Gods and Goddesses This book is about the mystery of neteru, the gods and goddesses of Ancient Egypt (Kamit, Kemet). Neteru means "Gods and Goddesses." But the Neterian teaching of Neteru represents more than the usual limited modern day concept of "divinities" or "spirits." The Neteru of Kamit are also metaphors, cosmic principles and vehicles for the enlightening teachings of Shetaut Neter (Ancient Egyptian-African Religion). Actually they are the elements for one of the most advanced systems of spirituality ever conceived in human history. Understanding the concept of neteru provides a firm basis for spiritual evolution and the pathway for viable culture, peace on earth and a healthy human society.   Why is it important to have gods and goddesses in our lives? In order for spiritual evolution to be possible, once a human being has accepted that there is existence after death and there is a transcendental being who exists beyond time and space knowledge, human beings need a connection to that which

239

transcends the ordinary experience of human life in time and space and a means to understand the transcendental reality beyond the mundane reality. ISBN: 1-884564-23-2    $21.95

31.    *EGYPTIAN MYSTERIES VOL. 3* The Priests and Priestesses of Ancient Egypt This volume details the path of Neterian priesthood, the joys, challenges and rewards of advanced Neterian life, the teachings that allowed the priests and priestesses to manage the most long lived civilization in human history and how that path can be adopted today; for those who want to tread the path of the Clergy of Shetaut Neter. ISBN: 1-884564-53-4 $24.95

32.    *The War of Heru and Set:* The Struggle of Good and Evil for Control of the World and The Human Soul This volume contains a novelized version of the Asarian Resurrection myth that is based on the actual scriptures presented in the Book Asarian Religion (old name –Resurrecting Osiris). This volume is prepared in the form of a screenplay and can be easily adapted to be used as a stage play. Spiritual seeking is a mythic journey that has many emotional highs and lows, ecstasies and depressions, victories and frustrations. This is the War of Life that is played out in the myth as the struggle of Heru and Set and those are mythic characters that represent the human Higher and Lower self. How to understand the war and emerge victorious in the journey o life? The ultimate victory and fulfillment can be experienced, which is not changeable or lost in time. The purpose of myth is to convey the wisdom of life through the story of divinities who show the way to overcome the challenges and foibles of life. In this volume the feelings and emotions of the characters of the myth have been highlighted to show the deeply rich texture of the Ancient Egyptian myth. This myth contains deep spiritual teachings and insights into the nature of self, of God and the mysteries of life and the means to discover the true meaning of life and thereby achieve the true purpose of life. To become victorious in the battle of life means to become the King (or Queen) of Egypt.Have you seen movies like The Lion King, Hamlet, The Odyssey, or The Little Buddha? These have been some of the most popular movies in modern times. The Sema Institute of Yoga is dedicated to researching and presenting the wisdom and culture of ancient Africa.  The Script is designed to be produced as a motion picture but may be

addapted for the theater as well. $21.95    copyright 1998 By Dr. Muata Ashby ISBN 1-8840564-44-5

33.    *AFRICAN DIONYSUS: FROM EGYPT TO GREECE:* The Kamitan Origins of Greek Culture and Religion ISBN: 1-884564-47-X FROM EGYPT TO GREECE    This insightful manual is a reference to Ancient Egyptian mythology and philosophy and its correlation to what later became known as Greek and Rome mythology and philosophy. It outlines the basic tenets of the mythologies and shoes the ancient origins of Greek culture in Ancient Egypt. This volume also documents the origins of the Greek alphabet in Egypt as well as Greek religion, myth and philosophy of the gods and goddesses from Egypt from the myth of Atlantis and archaic period with the Minoans to the Classical period. This volume also acts as a resource for Colleges students who would like to set up fraternities and sororities based on the original Ancient Egyptian principles of Sheti and Maat philosophy. ISBN: 1-884564-47-X $22.95 U.S.

**34.**    *THE FORTY TWO    PRECEPTS OF MAAT,    THE PHILOSOPHY OF    RIGHTEOUS ACTION AND THE ANCIENT EGYPTIAN WISDOM TEXTS* ADVANCED STUDIES This manual is designed for use with the 1998 Maat Philosophy Class conducted by Dr. Muata Ashby. This is a detailed study of Maat Philosophy. It contains a compilation of the 42 laws or precepts of Maat and the corresponding principles which they represent along with the teachings of the ancient Egyptian Sages relating to each. Maat philosophy was the basis of Ancient Egyptian society and government as well as the heart of Ancient Egyptian myth and spirituality. Maat is at once a goddess, a cosmic force and a living social doctrine, which promotes social harmony and thereby paves the way for spiritual evolution in all levels of society. ISBN: 1-884564-48-8  $16.95 U.S.

**35.    *THE SECRET LOTUS: Poetry of Enlightenment***
Discover the mystical sentiment of the Kemetic teaching as expressed through the poetry of Sebai Muata Ashby. The teaching of spiritual awakening is uniquely experienced when the poetic sensibility is present. This first volume contains the poems written between 1996 and 2003. **1-884564--16 -X $16.99**

### 36. The Ancient Egyptian Buddha: The Ancient Egyptian Origins of Buddhism

This book is a compilation of several sections of a larger work, a book by the name of African Origins of Civilization, Religion, Yoga Mysticism and Ethics Philosophy. It also contains some additional evidences not contained in the larger work that demonstrate the correlation between Ancient Egyptian Religion and Buddhism. This book is one of several compiled short volumes that has been compiled so as to facilitate access to specific subjects contained in the larger work which is over 680 pages long. These short and small volumes have been specifically designed to cover one subject in a brief and low cost format. This present volume, The Ancient Egyptian Buddha: The Ancient Egyptian Origins of Buddhism, formed one subject in the larger work; actually it was one chapter of the larger work. However, this volume has some new additional evidences and comparisons of Buddhist and Neterian (Ancient Egyptian) philosophies not previously discussed. It was felt that this subject needed to be discussed because even in the early 21st century, the idea persists that Buddhism originated only in India independently. Yet there is ample evidence from ancient writings and perhaps more importantly, iconographical evidences from the Ancient Egyptians and early Buddhists themselves that prove otherwise. This handy volume has been designed to be accessible to young adults and all others who would like to have an easy reference with documentation on this important subject. This is an important subject because the frame of reference with which we look at a culture depends strongly on our conceptions about its origins. in this case, if we look at the Buddhism as an Asiatic religion we would treat it and it's culture in one way. If we id as African [Ancient Egyptian] we not only would see it in a different light but we also must ascribe Africa with a glorious legacy that matches any other culture in human history and gave rise to one of the present day most important religious philosophies. We would also look at the culture and philosophies of the Ancient Egyptians as having African insights that offer us greater depth into the Buddhist philosophies. Those insights inform our knowledge about other African traditions and we can also begin to understand in a deeper way the effect of Ancient Egyptian culture on African culture and also on the Asiatic as well. We would also be able to discover the glorious and wondrous teaching of mystical philosophy that Ancient Egyptian Shetaut Neter religion offers, that is as powerful as any other mystic system of spiritual philosophy in the world today. ISBN: 1-884564-61-5    $28.95

**37. The Death of American Empire: Neo-conservatism, Theocracy, Economic Imperialism, Environmental Disaster and the Collapse of Civilization**

This work is a collection of essays relating to social and economic, leadership, and ethics, ecological and religious issues that are facing the world today in order to understand the course of history that has led humanity to its present condition and then arrive at positive solutions that will lead to better outcomes for all humanity. It surveys the development and decline of major empires throughout history and focuses on the creation of American Empire along with the social, political and economic policies that led to the prominence of the United States of America as a Superpower including the rise of the political control of the neo-con political philosophy including militarism and the military industrial complex in American politics and the rise of the religious right into and American Theocracy movement. This volume details, through historical and current events, the psychology behind the dominance of western culture in world politics through the "Superpower Syndrome Mandatory Conflict Complex" that drives the Superpower culture to establish itself above all others and then act hubristically to dominate world culture through legitimate influences as well as coercion, media censorship and misinformation leading to international hegemony and world conflict. This volume also details the financial policies that gave rise to American prominence in the global economy, especially after World War II, and promoted American preeminence over the world economy through Globalization as well as the environmental policies, including the oil economy, that are promoting degradation of the world ecology and contribute to the decline of America as an Empire culture. This volume finally explores the factors pointing to the decline of the American Empire economy and imperial power and what to expect in the aftermath of American prominence and how to survive the decline while at the same time promoting policies and social-economic-religious-political changes that are needed in order to promote the emergence of a beneficial and sustainable culture. **$25.95soft** 1-884564-25-9, Hard Cover **$29.95soft** 1-884564-45-3

**38. The African Origins of Hatha Yoga: And its Ancient Mystical Teaching**

The subject of this present volume, The Ancient Egyptian Origins of Yoga Postures, formed one subject in the larger works, African Origins of Civilization Religion, Yoga Mysticism and Ethics Philosophy and the Book Egypt and India is the section of the book African Origins of

Civilization. Those works contain the collection of all correlations between Ancient Egypt and India. This volume also contains some additional information not contained in the previous work. It was felt that this subject needed to be discussed more directly, being treated in one volume, as opposed to being contained in the larger work along with other subjects, because even in the early 21st century, the idea persists that the Yoga and specifically, Yoga Postures, were invented and developed only in India. The Ancient Egyptians were peoples originally from Africa who were, in ancient times, colonists in India. Therefore it is no surprise that many Indian traditions including religious and Yogic, would be found earlier in Ancient Egypt. Yet there is ample evidence from ancient writings and perhaps more importantly, iconographical evidences from the Ancient Egyptians themselves and the Indians themselves that prove the connection between Ancient Egypt and India as well as the existence of a discipline of Yoga Postures in Ancient Egypt long before its practice in India. This handy volume has been designed to be accessible to young adults and all others who would like to have an easy reference with documentation on this important subject. This is an important subject because the frame of reference with which we look at a culture depends strongly on our conceptions about its origins. In this case, if we look at the Ancient Egyptians as Asiatic peoples we would treat them and their culture in one way. If we see them as Africans we not only see them in a different light but we also must ascribe Africa with a glorious legacy that matches any other culture in human history. We would also look at the culture and philosophies of the Ancient Egyptians as having African insights instead of Asiatic ones. Those insights inform our knowledge bout other African traditions and we can also begin to understand in a deeper way the effect of Ancient Egyptian culture on African culture and also on the Asiatic as well. When we discover the deeper and more ancient practice of the postures system in Ancient Egypt that was called "Hatha Yoga" in India, we are able to find a new and expanded understanding of the practice that constitutes a discipline of spiritual practice that informs and revitalizes the Indian practices as well as all spiritual disciplines. $19.99 ISBN 1-884564-60-7

### 39. The Black Ancient Egyptians

This present volume, The Black Ancient Egyptians: The Black African Ancestry of the Ancient Egyptians, formed one subject in the larger work: The African Origins of Civilization, Religion, Yoga Mysticism and Ethics Philosophy. It was felt that this subject needed to be discussed because even in the early 21st century, the idea persists that the Ancient Egyptians were peoples originally from Asia Minor who came into North-East Africa. Yet there is ample evidence from ancient writings and perhaps more importantly, iconographical evidences from the Ancient Egyptians themselves that proves otherwise. This handy volume has been designed to be accessible to young adults and all others who would like to have an easy reference with documentation on this important subject. This is an important subject because the frame of reference with which we look at a culture depends strongly on our conceptions about its origins. in this case, if we look at the Ancient Egyptians as Asiatic peoples we would treat them and their culture in one way. If we see them as Africans we not only see them in a different light but we also must ascribe Africa with a glorious legacy that matches any other culture in human history. We would also look at the culture and philosophies of the Ancient Egyptians as having African insights instead of Asiatic ones. Those insights inform our knowledge bout other African traditions and we can also begin to understand in a deeper way the effect of Ancient Egyptian culture on African culture and also on the Asiatic as well. ISBN 1-884564-21-6 $19.99

### 40. The Limits of Faith: The Failure of Faith-based Religions and the Solution to the Meaning of Life

Is faith belief in something without proof? And if so is there never to be any proof or discovery? If so what is the need of intellect? If faith is trust in something that is real is that reality historical, literal or metaphorical or philosophical? If knowledge is an essential element in faith why should there by so much emphasis on believing and not on understanding in the modern practice of religion? This volume is a compilation of essays related to the nature of religious faith in the context of its inception in human history as well as its meaning for religious practice and relations between religions in modern times. Faith has come to be regarded as a virtuous goal in life. However, many people have asked how can it be that an endeavor that is supposed to be dedicated to spiritual upliftment has led to more conflict in human history than any other social factor? ISBN 1884564631 SOFT COVER - $19.99, ISBN 1884564623 HARD COVER -$28.95

### 41. Redemption of The Criminal Heart Through Kemetic Spirituality and Maat Philosophy

Special book dedicated to inmates, their families and members of the Law Enforcement community. ISBN: 1-884564-70-4
$5.00

### 42. COMPARATIVE MYTHOLOGY

What are Myth and Culture and what is their importance for

understanding the development of societies, human evolution and the search for meaning? What is the purpose of culture and how do cultures evolve? What are the elements of a culture and how can those elements be broken down and the constituent parts of a culture understood and compared? How do cultures interact? How does enculturation occur and how do people interact with other cultures? How do the processes of acculturation and cooptation occur and what does this mean for the development of a society? How can the study of myths and the elements of culture help in understanding the meaning of life and the means to promote understanding and peace in the world of human activity? This volume is the exposition of a method for studying and comparing cultures, myths and other social aspects of a society. It is an expansion on the Cultural Category Factor Correlation method for studying and comparing myths, cultures, religions and other aspects of human culture. It was originally introduced in the year 2002. This volume contains an expanded treatment as well as several refinements along with examples of the application of the method. the apparent. I hope you enjoy these art renditions as serene reflections of the mysteries of life. ISBN: 1-884564-72-0
Book price $21.95

### 43. CONVERSATION WITH GOD: Revelations of the Important Questions of Life
**$24.99 U.S.**

This volume contains a grouping of some of the questions that have been submitted to Sebai Dr. Muata Ashby. They are efforts by many aspirants to better understand and practice the teachings of mystical spirituality. It is said that when sages are asked spiritual questions they are relaying the wisdom of God, the Goddess, the Higher Self, etc. There is a very special quality about the Q & A process that does not occur during a regular lecture session. Certain points come out that would not come out otherwise due to the nature of the process which ideally occurs after a lecture. Having been to a certain degree enlightened by a lecture certain new questions arise and the answers to these have the effect of elevating the teaching of the lecture to even higher levels. Therefore, enjoy these exchanges and may they lead you to enlightenment, peace and prosperity. Available Late Summer 2007 ISBN: 1-884564-68-2

### 44. MYSTIC ART PAINTINGS
(with Full Color images) This book contains a collection of the small number of paintings that I have created over the years. Some were used as early book covers and others were done simply to express certain spiritual feelings; some were created for no purpose except to express the joy of color and the feeling of relaxed freedom. All are to elicit mystical awakening in the viewer. Writing a book on philosophy is like

sculpture, the more the work is rewritten the reflections and ideas become honed and take form and become clearer and imbued with intellectual beauty. Mystic music is like meditation, a world of its own that exists about 1 inch above ground wherein the musician does not touch the ground. Mystic Graphic Art is meditation in form, color, image and reflected image which opens the door to the reality behind the apparent. I hope you enjoy these art renditions and my reflections on them as serene reflections of the mysteries of life, as visual renditions of the philosophy I have written about over the years. ISBN 1-884564-69-0    $19.95

## 45. ANCIENT EGYPTIAN HIEROGLYPHS FOR BEGINNERS

This brief guide was prepared for those inquiring about how to enter into Hieroglyphic studies on their own at home or in study groups. First of all you should know that there are a few institutions around the world which teach how to read the Hieroglyphic text but due to the nature of the study there are perhaps only a handful of people who can read fluently. It is possible for anyone with average intelligence to achieve a high level of proficiency in reading inscriptions on temples and artifacts; however, reading extensive texts is another issue entirely. However, this introduction will give you entry into those texts if assisted by dictionaries and other aids. Most Egyptologists have a basic knowledge and keep dictionaries and notes handy when it comes to dealing with more difficult texts. Medtu Neter or the Ancient Egyptian hieroglyphic language has been considered as a "Dead Language." However, dead languages have always been studied by individuals who for the most part have taught themselves through various means. This book will discuss those means and how to use them most efficiently. ISBN 1884564429 **$28.95**

## 46. ON THE MYSTERIES: Wisdom of An Ancient Egyptian Sage -with Foreword by Muata Ashby

This volume, On the Mysteries, by Iamblichus (Abamun) is a unique form or scripture out of the Ancient Egyptian religious tradition. It is written in a form that is not usual or which is not usually found in the remnants of Ancient Egyptian scriptures. It is in the form of teacher and disciple, much like the Eastern scriptures such as Bhagavad Gita or the Upanishads. This form of writing may not have been necessary in Ancient times, because the format of teaching in Egypt was different prior to the conquest period by the Persians, Assyrians, Greeks and later the Romans. The question and answer format can be found but such extensive discourses and corrections of misunderstandings within the context of a teacher - disciple relationship is not usual. It therefore provides extensive insights into the times when it was written and the state of practice of Ancient Egyptian and other mystery religions. This has important implications for our times because we are today, as in the Greco-Roman period, also besieged with varied religions and new age philosophies as well as social strife and war. How can we understand our times and also make sense of the forest of spiritual traditions? How can we cut through the cacophony of religious fanaticism, and ignorance as well as misconceptions about the mysteries on the other in order to discover the true purpose of religion and the secret teachings that open up the mysteries of life and the way to enlightenment and immortality? This book, which comes to us from so long ago, offers us transcendental wisdom that applied to the world two thousand years ago as well as our world today. ISBN 1-884564-64-X    $25.95

### 47. The Ancient Egyptian Wisdom Texts -Compiled by Muata Ashby

The Ancient Egyptian Wisdom Texts are a genre of writings from the ancient culture that have survived to the present and provide a vibrant record of the practice of spiritual evolution otherwise known as religion or yoga philosophy in Ancient Egypt. The principle focus of the Wisdom Texts is the cultivation of understanding, peace, harmony, selfless service, self-control, Inner fulfillment and spiritual realization. When these factors are cultivated in human life, the virtuous qualities in a human being begin to manifest and sinfulness, ignorance and negativity diminish until a person is able to enter into higher consciousness, the coveted goal of all civilizations. It is this virtuous mode of life which opens the door to self-discovery and spiritual enlightenment. Therefore, the Wisdom Texts are important scriptures on the subject of human nature, spiritual psychology and mystical philosophy. The teachings presented in the Wisdom Texts form the foundation of religion as well as the guidelines for conducting the affairs of every area of social interaction including commerce, education, the army, marriage, and especially the legal system. These texts were sources for the famous 42 Precepts of Maat of the Pert M Heru (Book of the Dead), essential regulations of good conduct to develop virtue and purity in order to attain higher consciousness and immortality after death.  ISBN1-884564-65-8    $18.95

### 48. THE KEMETIC TREE OF LIFE
THE KEMETIC TREE OF LIFE: Newly Revealed Ancient Egyptian Cosmology and Metaphysics for Higher Consciousness

The Tree of Life is a roadmap of a journey which explains how Creation came into being and how it will end. It also explains what Creation is composed of and also what human beings are and what they are composed of. It also explains the process of Creation, how Creation develops, as well as who created Creation and where that entity may be found. It also explains how a human being may discover that entity and in so doing also discover the secrets of Creation, the meaning of life and the means to break free from the pathetic condition of human limitation and mortality in order to discover the higher realms of being by discovering the principles, the levels of existence that are beyond the simple physical and material aspects of life. This book contains color plates  **ISBN: 1-884564-74-7**
**$27.95 U.S.**

## Order Form

Telephone orders: Call Toll Free: 1(305) 378-6253. Have your AMEX, Optima, Visa or MasterCard ready.

Fax orders: 1-(305) 378-6253      E-MAIL ADDRESS:
Semayoga@aol.com

Postal Orders: Sema Institute of Yoga, P.O. Box 570459, Miami, Fl. 33257. USA.

Please send the following books and / or tapes.

ITEM

_____Cost $_____
_____Cost $_____
_____Cost $_____
_____Cost $_____
_____Cost $_____

Total

$_____

Name:_____

Physical Address:_____

City:_____ State:_____ Zip:_____

Sales tax: Please add 6.5% for books shipped to Florida addresses
_____Shipping: $6.50 for first book and .50¢ for each additional
_____Shipping: Outside US $5.00 for first book and $3.00 for each additional

_____Payment:_____
_____Check -Include Driver License #:

_____

_____Credit card: _____ Visa, _____ MasterCard, _____ Optima,
_____ AMEX.

Card number:_____
Name on card:_____ Exp.
date:_____/_____

**Copyright 1995-2005 Dr. R. Muata Abhaya Ashby**
**Sema Institute of Yoga**
**P.O.Box 570459, Miami, Florida, 33257**
(305) 378-6253 Fax: (305) 378-6253

www.ingramcontent.com/pod-product-compliance
Lightning Source LLC
Chambersburg PA
CBHW072102020426
42334CB00017B/1601